CENSORSHIP: EVIDENCE OF BIAS IN OUR CHILDREN'S TEXTBOOKS

Censorship: Evidence of Bias in Our Children's Textbooks

Paul C. Vitz

SERVANT BOOKS
Ann Arbor, Michigan

Cover design: Michael Andaloro
Cover photograph: Howard M. DeCruyenaere

Published by Servant Books
P.O. Box 8617
Ann Arbor, Michigan 48107

Printed in the United States of America
ISBN 0-89283-305-X

For Carl Horn and Stephen Galebach

Table of Contents

Figures

Tables

Preface

THE RESEARCH DESCRIBED HERE WAS FUNDED by the federal government through the major federal agency that supports education research, the National Institute of Education (NIE). The NIE is now part of the Department of Education. The final technical report was completed in September 1985 and is available from the government on the ERIC system for a nominal fee. The study was done at New York University for the government, but obviously not by the government. Thus, the findings reported here are neither approved nor disapproved by the government itself. This policy is the case for virtually all government-supported research projects.

All of the results from the original report of the textbook study are included here. Also included are a few additional analyses of the results; considerable extra interpretation and context; and a few responses to criticisms of the research that came to my attention after the study was completed.

Before I even began research on this project, I was surprised by the amount of partisan political opposition to its funding. Although I was able to stay out of most of the political controversy, I received firsthand reports about the struggle. Very simply, it was clear that the deeply entrenched liberal education establishment did not want to fund any research capable of challenging their views. The education establishment, unable to see the obvious ideological character of their position, claimed that this project was politicizing education and education research.

The present study appears to be the only systematic study of religion and traditional values in a representative sample of the country's public school textbooks. However, there have been several earlier but small scale reports on the same or related topics. As part of the NIE project, Professor Donald Oppewal summarized the relevant previously published material. His summary can be found as Appendix A, and the reader of Oppewal's report will see that the findings of these earlier and much less systematic studies reliably support the results reported here. Another quite recent study showing the same bias in the material used in high school literature classes is Bryce J. Christensen's insightful essay reprinted in Appendix B.

The primary focus of chapters 2-5 is on the research project itself: How it was conducted, what textbooks were evaluated, and what was found. There is little that one can do to describe a research study in an especially dramatic or fascinating style. But I hope that the project is presented clearly and that the results themselves will be found intrinsically interesting.

Acknowledgements

MY MAJOR DEBT IS TO TWO YOUNG LAWYERS, Carl Horn III (University of South Carolina, 1976) and Stephen Galebach (Harvard University, 1979). It was they who wrote the proposal for what eventually became the present project. While later, again, it was their skills at persuasion that led me to accept the job as the project principal investigator. In spite of my reluctance they certainly turned out to be right, for the study was more than worth the time and effort. So my special thanks go to Carl and Steve.

I am also indebted to Edward A. Wynne who provided, throughout the project, much needed encouragement, information, and advice. Donald Oppewal also added his important expertise to the project. Likewise, Henrietta Schwartz contributed to the total project. These educators do not necessarily agree with all of the positions stated here but their professional competence and wisdom was greatly appreciated.

Several people contributed in their capacity as critics and representatives, if you will, of the honest opposition. Especially helpful was Arthur Woodward of EPIE (Educational Products Information Exchange, an independent research corporation specializing in education research). His critical and somewhat jaundiced eye was indispensable. Likewise, thanks are due to Arthur's California EPIE colleague Cathleen Carter Nagel, who supervised the outside, independent evaluations of much of the study. (Both Drs. Woodward and Carter Nagel have left EPIE and are now part of a new company specializing in textbook evaluation.)

I also very much appreciated the help of my primary National Institute of Education (NIE) project officer Grace Mastalli. Although this research was part of a considerable political storm at NIE, Grace was always calm, patient, efficient, and fair. Would that all our relations with the federal government were so edifying.

ONE

Censorship in Public School Textbooks: An Overview

THE STUDY DESCRIBED HERE was conducted to answer some important and basic questions. Are public school textbooks biased? Are they censored? The answer to both is yes. And the nature of the bias is clear: Religion, traditional family values, and conservative political and economic positions have been reliably excluded from children's textbooks. This exclusion is particularly disturbing because it is found in a system paid for by taxpayers, and one that claims, moreover, to be committed to impartial knowledge and accuracy.

In spite of the biases such as those that are described here there is no evidence of any kind of conscious conspiracy operating to censor textbooks. Instead, a very widespread secular and liberal mindset appears to be responsible. This mindset pervades the leadership in the world of education (and textbook publishing) and a secular and liberal bias is its inevitable consequence.

In the first part of the project a total of sixty representative social studies textbooks were carefully evaluated. In grades 1 through 4 these books introduce the child to U.S. society—to family life, community activities, ordinary economic trans-actions, and some history. None of the books covering grades 1 through 4 contain one word referring to any religious activity in contemporary American life. For example, not one word refers to any child or adult who prayed, or who went to church or temple. The same was true for the twenty grade 5 and 6 texts, as well. An occasional rare picture (without captions) in these sixty books does depict Jewish, Catholic, Amish, or vague nondenominational religious scenes. The few pictures, all told there were only eleven, that do refer to religious activity were distributed over sixty books and roughly 15,000 pages. In any case, not one word or image in any book shows any form of contemporary representative Protestantism.

In a very general way the family is often mentioned in the textbooks, but the idea that marriage is the origin and foundation of the family is never presented. Indeed, the words *marriage, wedding, husband, wife,* do not occur once in these books. Nowhere is it suggested that being a mother or homemaker was a worthy and important role for a woman.

The fifth grade U.S. history texts include modest coverage of religion in colonial America and in the early Southwest missions; however, the treatment of the past 100 or 200 years is so devoid of reference to religion as to give the impression that it has almost ceased to exist in America. The sixth grade books deal with world history or world culture, and they neglect, often to the point of serious distortion, Jewish and Christian historical contributions.

Social studies books frequently select individuals to serve as "role models," that is, to represent important, admirable Americans. Such figures are given a photo and special coverage of their lives. For grades 1 through 6, a total of twenty-three role models who had political or ideological significance for U.S. society since World War II were identified. Typical selections include Eleanor Roosevelt, Martin Luther King, Jr., Margaret Mead, Rachel Carson, and Los Angeles Mayor Tom Bradley. Only one of the role models (Clare Booth Luce) is a conservative. Most of the role models are Democrats and the few Republicans (former Rep. Millicent Fenwick and Sen. Nancy Kassebaum) are women. Not one contemporary role model is conservative and male, and no person from business since World War II was selected.

High school books covering U.S. history were also studied, and none came close to adequately presenting the major religious events of the past 100 to 200 years. Most disturbing was the constant omission of reference to the large role that religion has always played in American life. This fact has been seen as a fundamental feature of American society by foreign observers since de Tocqueville.

A total of 670 stories and articles from grades 3 and 6 were also analyzed. A very small number of stories have religion as a secondary theme, but no story features Christian or Jewish religious motivation, although one story does make American Indian religion the central theme in the life of an American white girl. Again, there was not one reference to Protestant religious life.

Another notable finding is that business was ignored. No Horatio Alger stories appear in these readers. No story features an immigrant who makes good in America in business or in a profession. Almost no story features marriage or motherhood as important or positive, nor does any story give any positive significance to babies. But there are many aggressively feminist stories that openly deride traditional manhood.

Some particular examples of the bias against religion are significant. One social studies book has thirty pages on the Pilgrims, including the first Thanksgiving. But there is not one word (or image) that referred to religion as even a part of the Pilgrims' life. One mother whose son is in a class using this book wrote me to say that he came home and told her that "Thanksgiving was when the Pilgrims gave thanks to the Indians." The mother called the principal of this suburban New York City school to point out that Thanksgiving was when the Pilgrims thanked God. The principal responded by saying "that was her opinion"—the schools could only teach what was in the books!

Another social studies text has a page on Joan of Arc in which there was no reference to *any* religious aspect of her life. This is an obvious serious misrepresentation of her historical meaning. (Apparently Joan of Arc was included because she was a woman of historical importance.)

Another example is provided by a story of the Nobel laureate and Jewish writer Isaac Bashevis Singer. In his original story the main character, a boy, prayed "to God" and later remarked "Thank God." In the story as presented in the sixth grade reader the words "to God" were taken out and the expression "Thank

God" was changed to "Thank goodness." These changes not only represent a clear case of removing God from our textbooks, but they also transform the story. That is, by removing God, the spiritual dimension is taken out, and the story's clear answer to the boy's prayer is blunted or negated; and, of course, the historical accuracy of the author's portrayal of small town Jewish life in Eastern Europe is also falsified.

Many other examples of bias like those just mentioned are also described in the next four chapters.

I assume the reader already acknowledges that the content of school textbooks is important. The facts, interpretations, and values taught today's children will largely determine the character of tomorrow's citizenry. Indeed, it has been said that to control the content of a nation's textbooks is to control that nation's future. This, of course, is too extreme a statement since children learn much from sources other than textbooks. Nevertheless, C.S. Lewis was certainly right when he wrote, as the first sentence of his *Abolition of Man*, "I doubt whether we are sufficiently attentive to the importance of elementary textbooks." I know I was not sufficiently attentive until this project forced me to take a careful look. What I saw has certainly roused me from my educational slumber. It may do the same for you.

TWO

Bias in Social Studies— Grades 1-4

L ET'S BEGIN WITH A MORE DETAILED DESCRIPTION of the bias by looking at how religion is represented in the typical social studies textbooks used in the nation's public schools. Related issues such as the treatment of the family and of political issues will be addressed in the next chapter. What we will see is how little religion is contained in these books supposedly designed to tell the child the basic facts about American life.

Social Studies Textbooks: Sample Selection

It is important that the sample of books on which the results are based be carefully described and fairly chosen. For the reader especially interested in method, in particular textbooks or publishers, this section is indispensable. However, readers primarily interested in the results may wish to skip ahead to the results section.

The ten sets of six books that were selected are listed in Table 1 by publisher and copyright date. Also given in Table 1 are the states that have approved the text by putting it on their list of officially adopted or approved texts. The ten-set sample was selected as follows: (1) All social studies texts adopted by the states of California and Texas were included.[1] These two states were selected because of their large school age populations and because many other states look to their adoption lists for guidance in selecting their own texts. (2) In addition, any other texts adopted by both the states of Georgia and Florida were included.[2] This resulted in the ten sets listed in Table 1. We would have selected books from states in the Northeast, but none of these states has official adoption lists. Thus, the books actually used in such states depend on local choices.

Each publisher's name in Table 1 refers to a series set of six texts covering grades 1-6. The complete list of titles of all six texts for each publisher listed in Table 1 is given in Table D-1 in Appendix D.

This sample of ten sets is very representative of the nation as a whole. It includes first, as noted, all the social studies texts approved for use in California and Texas. These two states account, respectively, for 9.9% and 7.0% of the United States student population[3]; that is, 16.9% of the total student population. The official adoption lists of fifteen other states were also sent to me by EPIE (Educational Products Information Exchange): Alabama, Arkansas, Florida, Georgia, Idaho, Indiana, Mississippi, New Mexico, Nevada, North Carolina, Oklahoma, Oregon, South Carolina, Utah, and Virginia. (There are more states with social studies adoption lists, but only these fifteen responded to EPIE in time for the study's analysis. There is no reason to think the nonresponding adoption states are any different from those used here. The list of ten sets of texts in Table 1 accounts on the average for 71% of the texts on the fifteen states' adoption lists. Generalizing from these states to the rest of the country, the sample represents approximately 71% of the texts used outside of California and Texas. That is, 71% is an estimate of the proportion of students in all states except California and Texas that use the texts in this sample. Since we cover all the texts approved for use in California and Texas, one estimate is that (almost) 88% of the nation's students use the books in the study's sample. This estimate is probably high and needs qualification. It is possible that states that do not officially

Table 1

Publishers, copyright dates, and adoption states of the ten social studies textbook sets used in Studies one, two, and three. Further information on the sample of sixty books, each set covering grades 1-6, is listed in Appendix D, Table D-1.

Publisher and Copyright	Adoption States*
1. Allyn & Bacon (formerly Follett)—1983	CA, TX, and by AL, GA, IN, NC, NM, OR, VA
2. D.C. Heath (formerly American Book Co.)—1982	FL, GA, and by AL, AR, ID, IN, NM, NV, OK, OR, VA
3. Holt, Rinehart & Winston—1983	CA, and by ID, NC, OR
4. Laidlaw Brothers—1983	TX, and by AL, AR, FL, GA, ID, IN, MS, NM, NV, OK, OR, SC
5. Macmillan—1982-1983	CA, TX, and by AL, AR, GA, MS, NC, NM, OK, UT, VA
6. McGraw-Hill—1983	CA, and by GA, ID, NC, NM, NV, OK, OR, VA
7. Riverside (formerly Rand McNally)—1982	FL, GA, and by AL, ID, NC, NM, NV, OK, OR
8. Scott, Foresman & Co.—1983	CA, and by AL, AR, FL, GA, ID, IN, MS, NM, NV, OK, OR, SC, UT, VA
9. Silver Burdett—1984	CA, TX, and by AL, AR, FL, GA, ID, IN, NC, NM, OK, OR, UT
10. Steck-Vaughn (formerly Scholastic)—1983	CA, TX, and by AL, GA, MS, NV, SC

*From list supplied by EPIE.

adopt textbooks are more varied in the books they use as compared to the seventeen states whose official adoption lists we used. This possibility is hard to judge since statistics on the books used by schools in nonadoption states are not available. But in fact there is not likely to be much difference between these states and the others since it is well known that approximately ten to fifteen publishers account for the overwhelming majority of the books used for any given subject. The Table 1 list has ten of these publishers, and due to the influence of California and Texas, the present sample of ten contains the larger social science sellers within the set of fifteen or so possible candidates. Thus, an estimate that the sample used here accounts for 60 to 70 percent of those used in the country seems reasonable, even conservative.

Are the few fairly commonly used texts that are not in the sample different in any important way from those in the sample? A quick survey of two sets of books not in the present sample showed very little difference from those in Table 1.

Two other qualifications about the sample need to be made. The books officially adopted by adoption states sometimes have slightly different copyright dates (usually a few years earlier) as compared to the books used in this sample. The big publishers usually update in minor ways their social studies textbooks every two or three years, while adoption states may wait five or six years between official adoptions. Thus some states may be using a slightly earlier version of the books studied here. The differences between a book with the same title and authors but a slightly different edition (copyright) are small and would not affect the generality of the findings based on the Table 1 sample.

The adoption lists often change every few years and sometimes the complete list of books is not sent when requested. For example, I have learned that the Alabama list of state adoptions sent to me by EPIE omitted some texts. Thus, I do not claim that the percentages of state adoptions given here are perfectly accurate. However, I do claim that the books in this study definitely represent a very significant sample of the books used in the country, and in particular in the states shown in Tables 1 and 1-A, because the sample in Table 1 represents a large proportion of the nation's largest social science publishers. I have not come across any other study of content in textbooks that has used nearly as large or as representative a sample.

General Characteristics of the Sampled Books

All of the ten sets of books in the sample (Table 1) turn out to have the same general structure or format. The grade 1 texts deal with the individual student in the family and school setting; grade 2 texts expand the setting, usually to include the student's neighborhood; grade 3 broadens the context further to include the life of the surrounding community, e.g., town or city; and grade 4 includes the different possible regions of the country or sometimes world regions. These grade 4 texts are a kind of geography text mixed with stories about the life of the people in a given region. All three grade 4 texts are rather similar to the *National Geographic Magazine* in treatment; those that cover regions of the world give some emphasis to regions of the United States as well.

The books for these first four grades also include aspects of United States history or world culture. Because of the homogeneity of the sets for first four grades, they are analyzed together. The grade 5 texts are all introductions to United States history, and grade 6 texts are all introductions to world history or to world cultures. The analyses of the grade 5 and grade 6 books are each treated separately below.

The Purpose of Social Studies in Textbooks

Throughout this section the reader should keep in mind what social studies is about and why it is taught. The major purpose of social studies is to introduce the child to American social, economic, and political life as it exists today. In addition, especially in the fifth grade, social studies introduces the child to American history, to the important facts and topics of our past. Furthermore, reports and research show that the textbook is extremely important in determining what is taught in the classroom and that teacher dependence on the textbook has been growing in recent years.[4]

Study One: Religion in Social Studies Textbooks: Grades 1-4

Scoring. Every page of each book was read and any reference to religion was scored as a text item if it was made with words, and as an image item if it occurred as a picture. *Primary religious* references are defined as those that refer by word or picture to religious activity, such as praying, going to church, participating in a religious ceremony, or giving religious instruction. *Secondary religious* references are those that refer to religion in some indirect way, such as the mention of the date a church was built; or a reference to a minister as part of the community; or the inclusion of a photograph of a church; or showing, as part of a treatment of different ethnic groups in the United States, a scene of the Amish in a buggy or of Jews by an Israeli parade-float.

Accuracy. The accuracy of the scoring of the different religious categories was checked by having the texts scored by independent scorers provided by EPIE (Educational Products Information Exchange). That is, EPIE provided a kind of external, independent audit of the results. EPIE is a kind of "consumer reports" of education and has been active in educational research for over twenty years. It has a board of distinguished advisers. The author had no previous personal connection to EPIE, nor does EPIE have any connection to politically conservative or religious organizations.

The summary score sheets of all books (grades 1-4) based on the observations by the author of the books themselves, were sent to the EPIE office in Berkeley, California, for an independent check. The external judges at EPIE noted any references to religion that were missed by the author. There were three external judges; each checked the author's scoring of three or four of the publishers, grades 1-4, in Table 1. Thus, all pages of all the texts were independently evaluated by three external judges. Two of the twenty-four examples of a primary reference to religion were missed by the author. These two are included in Table 2. It is therefore likely that Table 2 represents 100% or close to 100% of all such references in the sample. Of the seventy-six secondary religious references in Table 3, fifteen were detected by the outside judges, i.e., missed by the author. Since it is unlikely that many additional secondary references were missed by both judges, Table 3 contains all or close to all such references. As noted, any item missed by the author was included in the data for purposes of analysis. As mentioned above, religious items were scored as either primary or secondary. This distinction was made very reliably as the author and the outside judges agreed 100% of the time as to which of these two categories suited a given reference to religion. The summaries of all forty social studies textbooks for grades 1-4 can be found in Appendix B of the original report (now on ERIC or available from the author).

Results. Table 2 shows the frequency and type of each primary religious reference in the forty sample textbooks, grades 1-4. Tables 2 and D-2 (Appendix D) refer only to religion in the United States. References to religion elsewhere are not included here for several reasons: because the main purpose of these books is to introduce the child to American society, because the number of such references were small, and because the particular countries and cultures referred to varied greatly from book to book.

The first result is that not one of the forty books totaling ten thousand pages had one *text* reference to a primary religious activity occurring in representative contemporary American life. One book has a reference to the life of the Amish—a small, rural Protestant group whose distinctive way of life has not changed in centuries. It would be hard to argue that they are representative of Protestant life today.

Another possible reference is a story on a Spanish urban ghetto, "El Barrio." In this story the *complete* relevant text reads, "Religion is important for people in El Barrio. Churches have places for dances and sports events." This is not a primary reference to religion since no actual religious activity is described. Furthermore, this comment can easily be viewed as hostile since the text doesn't mention Christianity or Roman Catholicism, and the churches are noted only as places for fun and games, not as places for worship.

There are, however, a few *images* showing primary religious activity in a contemporary American setting. In the first grade texts, two images are Jewish (Holt, Rinehart & Winston; Steck-

Table 2

primary References to Religion in Social studies Texts Grades 1-4

(American History and Society Only)

Book (publisher)	Grade 1	
	Text	Image
1. American Book/Health 1982		
2. Allyn & Bacon 1983		
3. Holt, Rinehart & Winston 1983		Jewish light candles
4. Laidlaw 1983		
5. Macmillan 1982-83		
6. McGraw-Hill 1983		Priest (probably R.C.) teaches kids
7. Riverside 1982		
8. Scott, Foresman 1983		
9. Silver Burdett 1984		
10. Steck-Vaughn 1983		Jewish light candles

Grade 2		Grade 3		Grade 4	
Text	Image	Text	Image	Text	Image
			Pilgrims pray at Thanks-giving		
		Pilgrim went to worship	Pilgrims pray at Thanks-giving	Puritan	Puritan religious service
	Jew with yarmulke at grave		Rabbi rolling scroll; priest (R.C.) talking with children		
		Pilgrim reads Bible at Thanks-giving; Sp. priests to teach Christianity	Family at Thanks-giving praying		
		Amish believe Bible says work land, stay together, keep away from non-Amish		Mayflower passengers prayed; Pilgrims thanked God; Puritan girl's day: attended church	
	Thanks-giving family praying		Minister at sickbed	Fr. Serra & California missions (twice)	Photo of Fr. Serra
				Pilgrims prayed	

Vaughn), one is Catholic (McGraw-Hill), and there is a rather vaguely drawn picture of a minister or priest at a funeral. In grade 2 there is one Jewish image and a photograph of a family praying at a Thanksgiving dinner (nondenominational). Grade 3 primary religious images are a Catholic priest, a rabbi, a minister or priest (with collar) at a sick bed, and a family with heads bowed for Thanksgiving. The grade 4 texts have no primary religious images dealing with contemporary American society.

The results shown in Table 2 support the following rather startling conclusions: twenty-five of the forty books have no reference in either word or image to American religious activity in *any* form; of the fifteen books that have a primary religious reference, seven refer only to religious activity in the historical past, either Puritan or Spanish mission life. That is, these seven never refer to Americans engaged in religious activity more recently than two hundred years ago. Of the eight books having a picture of religion in America today, five books (six images) have a Jewish or Catholic reference. The total of ten images showing any kind of contemporary religious activity is spread over roughly ten thousand pages (forty books at an average of about 250 pages a book).

The secondary religious references, both text and image, are in Table 2 found in Appendix D, and they present a similar pattern to that shown in Table 2. For grade 1 there is a reference to God in the Pledge of Allegiance; other secondary images include a church noted on a local map, a boy in bed with a crucifix on the wall behind him (implicitly Catholic), two images of Christmas trees, and one of children dyeing Easter eggs. Since Christmas trees and dyeing eggs by themselves are found in many non-religious homes, their religious significance is ambiguous and minor. In grade 2 there is one text reference to the Amish, the Pledge of Allegiance is given twice (including the words "one nation, under God"), and in one instance the music and words of "America the Beautiful" are printed with "God shed his grace on thee"; there is also a text reference to a church building. Secondary religious images are pictures of churches, of the Amish people, six churches on local maps, and a photo, without a caption, of a wedding party with a cross in the background.

Secondary religious references in grade 3 texts cite religious leaders as being part of the community leadership; one text notes that Martin Luther King, Jr. was a minister; there are two references to church buildings, one to ministers being important service workers, and a reference to the Great Seal of the United States and the motto "He (God) has favored our work." Grade 3 secondary images include images of Spanish mission churches, one of a Catholic cathedral, one of some Amish.

Grade 4 secondary text references are to Marian Anderson who sang in a church choir when young, the Pledge of Allegiance, and one reference to a church building. Grade 4 secondary images are one image of a church, five of Spanish missions, and two photos of the Mormon Temple in Salt Lake City.

Secondary religious images, although more numerous, are still far from common. And again the great majority of these oblique references are to religion in the past, not in the present. Specifically, twenty-one of the forty texts have no text (not one word) even about secondary aspects of religion; nineteen have no secondary images of any kind, and ten, 25% of the books, do not have a secondary word or picture referring to religion in America.

Discussion. The most striking thing about these texts is the total absence of any primary religious *text* about typical contemporary American religious life. In particular, there is not one text reference to characteristic American Protestant religious life in these books.

As for primary images, the situation is slightly better. There are four image references to contemporary Jewish practice, two to contemporary Catholic life, and one to a man in clerical dress, described as a minister, visiting the sick. There are two images that might be either a priest or minister, and two non-denominational families with heads bowed for Thanksgiving dinner.

Of course, if one goes back in time to the Colonial Period there are some primary texts and images of a Protestant nature—but the New England Puritans no longer exist as such today, and representation of their religious life carries an ambiguous meaning for present-day children. In some respects the message is that religion is old-fashioned and only for those who are not up-to-date. For example, Holt, Rinehart & Winston (grade 4) has a two-page story on Peacham, Vermont. This small village has a beautiful old Puritan church which is featured in the story not as a center of religious life but because it is the center for a contemporary summer piano festival. The message that religion is old-fashioned is also carried by the treatment of Spanish missions and by the several references to the Amish.

In any case, today's powerful Protestant religious world of the Bible Belt, of the born-again Christians, of the fundamentalists and of the evangelicals, of the Moral Majority, of Billy Graham, Oral Roberts, Jerry Falwell, the TV evangelists (even Norman Vincent Peale)—this very American Protestant world representing millions of Americans—is without *one* reference in word or image in this sample of forty books. Even the world of mainline Protestantism or of the *Prairie Home Companion* is entirely omitted. (One wonders what provincial and secular worlds these textbook writers live in!)

The secondary religious texts and images give essentially the same results. Keep in mind that these social studies books are aimed at introducing the student to American society primarily as it exists today, with some information on how it existed in the past. For example, today's job world and the world of recreation and travel get heavy emphasis.

There is something of a minor emphasis on Jewish and Catholic religious life. This is not to say these books give any religion anything like its proportional significance, but it is interesting that when on occasion religion is referred to, then Jewish or Catholic or sometimes Amish or Mormon images occur. This is very curious indeed, and one could suggest a psychological motive behind the obvious censorship of religion in these books. Those responsible for these books appear to have a deep-seated fear of any form of active contemporary Christianity, especially serious, committed Protestantism. This fear could have led the authors to deny and suppress the importance of this kind of religion in American life. That is, for those responsible for these books, active Protestantism may be threatening and hence taboo. This thesis can be supported by the peculiar pattern of the few references to religion that do occur, that do break through the secular censorship process. Specifically, as one gets further away from the major threatening form of religion, i.e., fundamentalist and evangelical Protestantism, the repression weakens and a few more distant types of religion occasionally get reported.

Distance from the central severely repressed form of religion can be measured on at least three different dimensions. First, there can be distance in religious character. Thus, Judaism and Catholicism and the Amish are distant enough from fundamentalist Protestantism to be less threatening; therefore, these forms get relatively more of what little religious coverage there is. In addition, these forms of religion can be interpreted as typical of minorities—and, like all minorities, they receive a certain sympathy. This explains, for example, the text reference to El Barrio and not to a more mainstream type of American Catholicism—although, as noted, even in that reference the words *Christian* or *Catholic,* even words referring to any religious activity, are not mentioned. (The word *religion* has apparently become a euphemistic synonym for [and repression of] *Christian* or *Protestant* or *Catholic,* since none of these three words is used in these books in connection with any primary or secondary reference to religion in the United States; this taboo extends to *Christ* and *Jesus,* names that do not occur in any of these books' treatments of contemporary American life.)

Another dimension for distancing is time. Hence the references to Puritan life in the 1600s are allowed to include religious elements. Likewise the oft-pictured Catholic missions of the Southwest can be referred to without too much anxiety. After all, these religious ways of living are now long gone.

A third dimension of distance is one of culture and geography. As noted, Tables 2 and 3 record the religious references relevant only to the history of the United States from the Colonial Period to the present. The occasional references in these books to other countries, such as Mexico or France, or to the American Indian cultures, are not treated since the primary concern of this study is on how American life and history is represented. But it is worth noting that when these books do cover *other* societies, then religion gets a greater emphasis. Thus, many of the sets treat American Indian life prior to the arrival of Europeans. In the process, Indian religion often gets a sympathetic treatment. For example, Holt, Rinehart & Winston (grade 3, p. 56) describes a

Hopi rain dance and prayer; Scott, Foresman (grade 3, p. 71) a Pueblo Indian story about prayer and how the Earth Mother created corn for them. (Also see Macmillan grade 3, pp. 262-264).

Mexico, when treated, usually gets religious coverage. Thus, Laidlaw (grade 1 on pp. 47 and 128) explicitly notes "religious" celebrations, though neither Catholic or Christian are mentioned; Laidlaw (grade 4, p. 325) also notes the Christ of the Andes statue in discussing South America.

Or consider the following comment about Europe: "As you see, in Europe many people are religious" (grade 4, McGraw-Hill, p. 247). Such a statement is never made about the United States—although religion has always been extremely important in American life.

Also, consider the Allyn & Bacon series (grades 1-4), which along with Riverside has the weakest treatment of religion of the publishers in the study. There is one reference to a California mission in grade 3; the only other reference is to Mother Teresa of Calcutta (grade 3, p. 155). She gets a small picture and a discussion as winner of the 1979 Nobel Peace Prize. Being Catholic and living in India she is distant enough—according to the present analysis—not to raise a threat.

Other examples of the washing-out of religion are such explanations as, "Pilgrims are people who make long trips," or "Mardi Gras is the end of winter celebration" (Macmillan, grade 3, pp. 52 and 186). Or the fact that these books feature significant discussions of each of the following American cities: San Francisco, Santa Fe, Saint Paul, Saint Louis, Saint Augustine— but not one book mentions whom these cities are named after.

Although an atypical religion sometimes pops up at a distance from the central most taboo form of Protestantism, the dominant theme is the denial of religion as an important part of present-day American life. Sometimes the censorship becomes especially offensive. It is common in these books to treat Thanksgiving without explaining to whom the Pilgrims gave thanks. For example, Riverside (grade 2) has a lengthy section on the Pilgrims, pages 35-65. But the Pilgrims are described *entirely* without any reference to religion; thus at the end of their first year they "wanted to give thanks for all they had" (p. 60) so they had the first Thanksgiving. But no mention is made of the fact that it

Figure 2:1

was God they were thanking. This same type of thing is also done in Silver Burdett, grade 1, page 48, and in grade 2, page 143; likewise Steck-Vaughn, grade 4, page 111; American Book, grade 3, pages 150-156; Scott, Foresman, grade 1, page 124. One mother wrote me that her first grade son was told by his teacher that at Thanksgiving the Pilgrims gave thanks to the Indians![5] When she complained to the principal that Thanksgiving was a feast to thank God, the principal replied that her position "was just opinion and not documented fact," and therefore they could not teach it. The principal said that "they could only teach what was contained in the history books." Here the principal is so ignorant as to be professionally incompetent. But maybe he's just been reading the social studies texts. (The school in question is in an upper-middle class New York City suburb.)

The Pueblo can pray to Mother Earth—but Pilgrims can't be described as praying to God. And never are Christians described as praying to Jesus, either in the United States or elsewhere, in the present or even in the past, at least as far as these forty books are concerned.

Looking over all the publishers in Table 1, we can say that Allyn

& Bacon, 1983 and Riverside, 1982 are markedly without religious content. McGraw-Hill, 1983 and American Book, 1982 are almost as bad. Such books should be rejected out of hand on grounds of obvious religious prejudice. Prejudice is the appropriate word to describe the situation. If leaving black Americans out of textbooks is *rightly* seen as antiblack—as racism—then the suppression or omission of religion is antireligious prejudice. Although Holt is far from impressive, it has the least unsatisfactory treatment of religion in these grade 1-4 texts.

THREE

Bias in Social Studies— Grades 5 and 6

I N THIS CHAPTER we examine social studies texts for grades 5 and 6 to observe how these books treat religion, the traditional family, and political issues.

Study Two: Religion in Grade 5

All ten publishers' grade 5 texts are introductions to United States history covering the period from the early 1600s to about 1980. They also present American Indian life prior to the European discovery of America. Material on the period from 1492 to 1600 is also given. Some books also include material on Mexican and Canadian history, but this material is omitted here since, as previously noted, the present study is only concerned with American history and society. The only possible ambiguous religious reference with respect to American history is Hitler's persecution of the Jews (the Holocaust). Although this event, strictly speaking, is primarily German and European in character, it had considerable impact on America, and references to the Holocaust are noted with respect to the representation of Judaism.

Scoring. Every page of each book was read, and a brief summary of each reference to religion was made. (The summaries are in the original report.) Initially every reference was also to be scored as expressing a positive, negative, or neutral attitude toward religion, but since most of the references were neutral, no regular attempt was made to treat this aspect of references to religion. Instead the primary concern is *whether* religion is mentioned, and if so *what* characteristics are referred to.

Results. General summaries of how each text treats religion will be given first.

1. *American Book, 1982 (grade 5).* After many positive references to native American Indian religion (e.g., pp. 75, 81, 87, 89), the issue of Western religion in the United States is framed *entirely* in terms of gaining religious freedom, as in the reaction to Puritan religious restriction (e.g., pp. 126, 137). There is no mention, however, of Catholic or other recent religious schools as expressions of religious freedom. The last direct reference to religion is on page 221, and the last mention of pioneers and immigrants seeking religious freedom is on page 301. There is one indirect reference when Martin Luther King, Jr. is noted briefly as "a young minister" (p. 363). There is no direct reference to religion in American history in the last one hundred years; there is only this one indirect reference to King in the 1960s.

Some important treatment of Christianity is clearly anti-Christian. Consider the discussion of Spanish Christianity in Mexico and the Southwest.

—"Spaniards thought the Christian religion should be brought to the American Indians." (But mostly they came for *gold and glory*.) (p. 113)
—"Missionaries came too." ". . . priests wanted to convert American Indians to Christianity."
—They founded missions. "Missions served as trading posts and as churches for the Spaniards. The Indians often were forced to work on the missions. They had to work in the mines or on the farms run by Spaniards. How did the American Indians feel about these newcomers? Were they willing to work on Spanish farms and in Spanish mines? How did they feel about giving up their own religion and taking on a new one? Many of them accepted changes, afraid perhaps of Spanish weapons. But many others fought back" (pp. 116-117).

There is here no balanced discussion which would include the positive contributions of Christianity to the Indians, no critical comment on Indian religion—for example the prevalent custom of human sacrifice among Aztec Indians of Mexico. In short, this textbook is both biased and seriously deficient.

2. *Allyn & Bacon, 1983 (grade 5)*. This text starts its treatment of religion with reference to freedom of religion as an important American belief (p. 45). It goes on to present the Spanish and Catholic Colonial Period in a generally descriptive and balanced way (e.g., pp. 95, 105, 117, 118, 119, 128, 130). This text continues with a discussion of the Colonial Period, i.e., Puritans, William Penn and Quakers, Lord Baltimore and Maryland—a more or less standard description in the context of religious freedom. It mentions John Harvard, a Puritan minister, who helped establish Harvard University in the early 1600s (p. 137). The last reference in the text to religious activity in American history is to missionaries in the early 1800s who brought Christianity to Hawaii. Near the end of the text, there are two references to the American belief in freedom of religion today and to a 1964 law against religious discrimination.

There is one interesting image of the masthead of W.L. Garrison's paper *The Liberator* (circa 1845). This, the major paper of the Abolitionist movement, shows Jesus and a cross in its center with a black man praying to him. "Love thy neighbor as thyself" is on a ribbon around the central two figures. However, no text connects Christianity to the Abolitionist movement.

The last third of this book treats the contemporary United States by geographical region. This section consists mostly of geography and related topics. Religion is referred to once in these 180 pages—i.e., a small photo of the Mormon Tabernacle Choir, on page 400. The last text reference to religion as part of American history deals with a period over one hundred years ago.

3. *Holt, Rinehart & Winston, 1983 (grade 5)*. Although this text, like the rest, had the universal superficial treatment of all topics, it at least gave religion a reasonable number of references. For example, Holt mentions that the Abolitionist movement had links to religious belief. It also says that "Dr. King had deep religious beliefs"—the only one of the ten books that noted this important fact about Martin Luther King, Jr. (Although they

again avoid saying "Christian.") This book's treatment of Jewish contributions to American history was also better than that of the other nine books. However, like all the rest of these grade 5 books, actual religious events—such as the two great religious awakenings of 1740 and 1830, the urban revivals, the Holiness-Pentecostal movement, and the Born-Again movement—were avoided. And the great religious character and energy of American society was somehow overlooked.

4. *Laidlaw, 1983 (grade 5)*. This book has a fairly standard set of early references to religion. It places heavy emphasis on religious freedom in the 1600s and 1700s through mention of figures such as Roger Williams, Anne Hutchinson, Thomas Hooker, William Penn, and Lord Baltimore. There is a one-page biography of Anne Hutchinson. The last real reference to religion in this text is to the Quakers and to the California Missions, both in the 1700s. There is one reference to Hawthorne's writing in the early 1800s as deriving from the Puritan past. There is a reference near the end of the book (p. 247) to the Bill of Rights' guarantee of the freedom to go to the church of one's choice. But the last historical reference to religion in America is more than 150 years ago.

5. *McGraw-Hill, 1983 (grade 5)*. This text presents a fairly standard treatment of the Spanish discovery and settlement period, and of Pilgrim and Puritan New England. It does note the importance of the church for early New England. Roger Williams, Anne Hutchinson, and William Penn are treated with the standard religious freedom emphasis. But it has some rather unusual later references, e.g., a statement that missionaries were one type of pioneer in the West in the 1830-1840s; a quote from Sojourner Truth mentioning that only Jesus heard her; a reference (unique in these books) to Irish immigrants and anti-Catholic prejudice; a reference to the large Jewish immigration in the 1880-1890s and reference to Jews in 1950 as refugees who came for freedom of religion. Recent pictures included the Amish as a subculture; a Jewish family lighting candles for Sukkoth; and a photo of Episcopal monks worshipping together. This photo is the only primary religious image in all sixty social studies books which shows any actual contemporary Protestant religious life. Even this is quite atypical of Protestantism. Major religious

events, such as the Great Awakenings, are not mentioned in this text.

6. *Macmillan, 1982-1983 (grade 5)*. This is an extremely short text that tries to put American history in one hundred pages, plus a few pages on the history of different geographical regions. The whole book is so superficial that it is hard to single out religion for the inadequacy of its treatment; no doubt most major themes are poorly represented in this book. However, the last reference to religion in American history is to the Mormons settling in Utah—although there is a reference to the Holocaust in Germany during World War II.

7. *Riverside, 1982 (grade 5)*. This book presents a weak but fairly standard treatment of Spanish discovery and of French and Puritan settlements. The Colonial Period mentions Roger Williams, Anne Hutchinson, the Catholics in Maryland, the Quakers, and the Jews in Rhode Island—the latter reference being unusual. Except to say that Jews and Mennonites were part of the large group of immigrants to the United States and to note that Martin Luther King, Jr. was a minister, there is no reference to religion in American history in the last one hundred years. It does note Nazi persecution of Jews in World War II.

8. *Scott, Foresman, 1983 (grade 5)*. This text is one of the *slightly* better treatments of religion in American history, primarily because of the variety of anecdotal comments with a religious element, especially for the nineteenth century. It has a standard treatment of the Spanish period, the French, the Pilgrims, and the Puritans. In its treatment of the religious freedom issue, the text emphasizes Roger Williams, Anne Hutchinson, the Quakers, the Catholics, and the Jews in the Colonial Period. There is a story of Asher Levy getting his rights in New Amsterdam; the Texas-Mexico conflict is noted as partly a Protestant-Catholic conflict; there is a Jefferson quote on slavery, "I tremble when I remember God is just"; and there is a quote of a response to the 1930s depression, "God knows what they lived on." The text reflects, however, no understanding of the religious basis of much of American history per se. There is a reference to post-Civil War western boom towns having churches, along with opera houses, theaters, and music halls. There is also a reference to churches in

the Alabama bus boycott of 1960 and a reference to "God" on the tomb of the unknown soldier.

9. *Silver Burdett, 1984 (grade 5)*. This book treats the Spanish and French discovery periods in a standard way. Religion is mentioned as a neutral or positive element. Pilgrims and Puritans are noted as religious: "A pilgrim is one who travels for religious reasons." The religious freedom issue is treated in a standard way through mention of Roger Williams, Anne Hutchinson, Lord Calvert, and William Penn. George Washington is shown with his hand on the Bible at his presidential inauguration and is quoted as saying, "so help me God." There is reference to Fr. Serra, Fr. Kino, Lincoln's reading of the Bible, the Mormons settling Salt Lake, and the burning of schools and churches by the KKK in the 1860s and 1870s. It mentions Martin Luther King, Jr. as a preacher and shows a reference to God on his tombstone. No reference is made to the black churches in the Civil Rights movement. There are no references to such major religious events as the Great Awakenings.

10. *Steck-Vaughn, 1983 (grade 5)*. This book is rather weak in its treatment of the early Spanish period. It neglects the French discovery period. The mission period in the Southwest is given some coverage, however. There is a treatment of the New England Pilgrims and Puritans with a heavy emphasis on religious freedom, including its significance for Catholics and Jews. There is a brief story of a Jewish hero of the War of Independence. It mentions Sojourner Truth and her spreading of God's word, though the main emphasis in this reference is on women's rights. It refers to a woman settler in 1873 who signs a letter "yours in prayer." The text does make mention of Hitler's hatred and persecution of the Jews in World War II and Martin Luther King, Jr. as a young minister, but otherwise nothing is mentioned about religion in the last one hundred years, e.g., no reference to King's religious motivation or the black church's role in his career.

General Discussion

The overwhelming impression received from all these books is the superficiality of their treatment of just about everything.

These books are a *pastiche* of topics and images without any serious historical treatment of what might have been going on. Nevertheless, certain aspects of the abysmal coverage of religion deserve special emphasis. For example, not one book notes the extreme liveliness and great importance of religion in American life in general. This religious energy—which generated such religions as Shakers, Mormons, Christian Scientists, Jehovah's Witnesses, Seventh Day Adventists, and Black Muslims—is never noted.

There is not *one* reference in *any* of these books to such major religious events as the Salem Witch Trials; the Great Awakening of the 1740s; the great revivals of the 1830s and 1840s; the great urban Christian revivals of the 1870-90 period; the very important Holiness and Pentecostal movements around 1880-1910; the liberal and conservative Protestant split in the early twentieth century; or the Born-Again movement of the 1960s and 1970s. Religion in the twentieth century hardly figures at all in these books; the whole issue is seriously neglected. For example, Martin Luther King, Jr.'s religious motivation is noted in only one text and only one text mentions the black churches as important in King's Civil Rights movement.

In spite of these books' emphasis on religious freedom and tolerance, there is not one reference to the large Catholic school system or to the recent Christian school movement as an expression of religious freedom.

Frequency of Reference to Religion

All references to religion in the above texts dealing with the history of the United States (or of territory that would become part of the United States) were recorded on summary data sheets. (See original report.) These events have been grouped for each text by century, starting with the 1600s. (Events in the 1500s are not treated since they were given relatively little treatment and most of these events did not refer explicitly to parts of the New World that are in the United States.) Table 3 presents the summary findings. The most striking thing about this table is the extreme decline in references to religion as one goes from the 1600s to the present century. Indeed, there is almost a ten-fold

Table 3

Number of Pages with a Reference to Religion as Part of American History in Grade 5 United States History Social Studies Texts

(Observations are categorized as text or image references and by century.)

Book (publisher)	1600s Text	1600s Image	1700s Text	1700s Image	1800s Text	1800s Image	1900s Text	1900s Image	Total
1. American Book 1982	8	3	4	1	0	0	0	0	16
2. Allyn & Bacon 1983	12	2	0	1	1	1	1	1	19
3. Holt, Rinehart & Winston 1983	11	2	2	2	4	0	2	0	23
4. Laidlaw 1983	16	4	9	3	0	0	0	0	32
5. McGraw-Hill 1983	10	4	3	0	5	0	1	3	26
6. Macmillan 1982-1983	9	1	3	2	3	0	0	0	18
7. Riverside 1982	10	0	1	3	2	0	0	1	17
8. Scott, Foresman 1983	9	0	5	1	10	1	2	0	28
9. Silver Burdett 1984	10	1	9	1	5	1	0	0	27
10. Steck-Vaughn 1983	7	2	6	3	4	1	0	0	23
Total	102	19	42	17	34	4	6	5	
Grand Total (Text and Image)	121		59		38		11		

*Excludes references to Jews and Nazi Holocaust in Germany in World War II; however, see Table 4 for this information.

Figure 3:1

Percent of pages in fifth grade American history textbooks which have a reference to religion, in each century from 1600 to present.

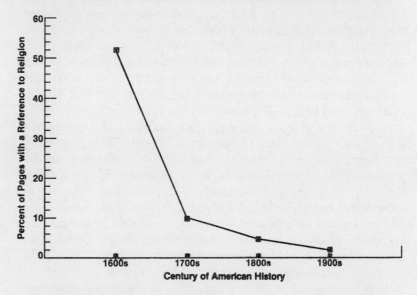

decrease in the number of such references. In fact, the decline is even more severe since these books have, on the average, many more pages covering the 1800s and the 1900s than for the earlier centuries. Thus, a more accurate measure of the decline in references to religion can be seen in Figure 3:1. This figure corrects for the number of pages of coverage for each century. For example, the average text has 24.5 pages covering the history of the 1600s, and the percentage (proportion) of these pages with reference to religion for 1600s is slightly over 50%. Figure 3:1 shows the percentage of pages covering each century that contain a reference to religion in this country in either text or image. In the 1700s this is 9.75% and in the 1800s, 3.42%. By the 1900s the percentage has dropped to 1.27 references every one hundred pages. (References to the Jewish Holocaust in Nazi Germany are not included in the later figure; they are, however, noted and discussed in the next section.)

Judaism

The treatment of Judaism in these books is extremely sporadic. Jewish contributions to American history have been important but, like those of many other religious groups, not well known. Five major Jewish aspects of American history are singled out here to measure how well Judaism is represented in these books: (1) the presence of Jews in America in the seventeenth and eighteenth centuries; (2) Jewish immigration into the United States in the 1880-1920 period; (3) the existence of anti-Jewish prejudice in the country, e.g., the Ku Klux Klan; (4) the significance of the Nazi Holocaust in World War II; and (5) a category for other references, especially any references to important Jewish-Americans such as Supreme Court Justice Brandeis. Technically speaking, the Nazi Holocaust is not part of American history per se but because of its intrinsic significance and because of its repercussion on much of American religious and political life it is included. In Table 4 the presence or absence of reference to these events is noted in each of the ten books in the sample. Some books, such as Holt, Rinehart & Winston, do relatively well. On the other hand, Allyn & Bacon and American Book continue their pathetic treatment of religion already observed in grades 1-4. Equally weak on Jewish contributions are Macmillan and Silver Burdett. Jewish religious practice is never described in the social studies texts which focus on the United States (i.e., grades 1-5). There are the four images noted in Table 2, but nothing about Jewish religious life per se is ever mentioned. By contrast, the religious beliefs and practices of the American Indians are given a moderate amount of attention—certainly much more than Jewish religious life. Recall also the references to American Indian religious practices scattered throughout the grade 1-4 social studies books.

Catholicism

The specific treatment of American Roman Catholicism is, if anything, even weaker than the coverage of Jewish-American contributions. Eight major Catholic aspects of American history are singled out to measure how well Catholic contributions are represented in these books: (1) the very significant early Catholic

Table 4

Fifth Grade Textbook Coverage of Important Jewish Aspects of American History

Textbook	Presence in Colonial Period	E. European Immigration	U.S. Prejudice Against KKK, Etc.	Holocaust Nazi-Persecution	Other	Percent Coverage
1. American 1982	p. 138					20
2. Allyn & Bacon 1983				pp. 284-5		20
3. Holt, Rinehart & Winston 1983	p. 78	p. 297	p. 329	pp. 347-8, 356	p. 393 Soviet Jews recent	100
4. Laidlaw 1983	p. 158			p. 412		40
5. McGraw-Hill 1983		pp. 240, 249 Emma Lazarus			p. 329 Recent Jewish immigrants	40
6. Macmillan* 1982-83				p. 135		20
7. Riverside 1982	p. 88	pp. 280-82		pp. 346, 348, 360		60
8. Scott, Foresman 1983	pp. 127-8	pp. 310-11		p. 359		60
9. Silver Burdett 1984				p. 231		20
10. Steck-Vaughn 1983	pp. 99, 121, 106-7	p. 320		pp. 366-7, 372		60

*This book treats American history proper in about one hundred pages, plus a few pages on the history of each United States geographical region; there is no index entry for Jewish, Judaism, etc.

settling of Florida, the Southwest, and California; (2) the Catholic presence in colonial America; (3) the intense anti-Catholic prejudice in the 1830-1865 period; (4) the establishment of the Catholic school system as a major expression of religious freedom; (5) the role of the Catholic church in assimilating so many immigrants from, for example, Ireland, Italy, Germany, Poland, and Lithuania; (6) the large number of Catholic hospitals, schools, and orphanages; (7) the anti-Catholic prejudice in twentieth century America, e.g., in the KKK and in the presidential elections involving Al Smith and John F. Kennedy; and (8) interesting and important Catholic personalities, e.g., Lord Baltimore, Elizabeth Seton, Orestes Brownson, Isaac Hecker, Mother Cabrini, Dorothy Day, Bishop Sheen, et al.

The coverage of Catholic contributions to American history can be described very simply: All texts have references (usually not extensive) to the first two events—both occurring in the 1700s or earlier; two books refer to anti-Catholic prejudice—McGraw-Hill in the mid-nineteenth century and Holt, Rinehart & Winston to the same in the twentieth century. Except for these two references, no book refers to items three through eight; and thus, Catholicism is for all practical purposes excluded from American history from 1800 to the present. That the Catholic school system was founded at great cost and sacrifice as an expression of the American search for religious freedom is not mentioned once. However, the religious freedom issue is the common theme that allows most of the references to religion in American colonial history. This oversight may be anti-Catholic prejudice, but it is also possible that it results from the present public school monopoly fearfully excluding any reference to an alternative system. No doubt the public schools are concerned that new Protestant schools using the same venerable religious freedom rationale have siphoned off hundreds of thousands of public school students in the last twenty years as Protestants have sought to pass on their faith and moral traditions to their children.

Study Three: Religion in Social Studies—Grade 6

The ten social studies texts for grade 6 all briefly cover either world history or world cultures combined with history. Because these books differ in the particular historical periods, countries, and cultures that are covered, it is hard to compare them systematically. However, some general observations, especially related to bias in the coverage of Judaism and Christianity, can be made.

Scoring. Each page of each book was read, and any reference to religion was briefly summarized. On the basis of this reading the following issues struck the author as important. These results, like the others, were evaluated for accuracy by EPIE.

1. *Neglect of Ancient and Modern Jewish History.* The early history of the Jews is of foundational significance to Western civilization—in many respects it is as important as ancient Greece and more important than ancient Egypt. However, there is far less coverage of Jewish history and religion than of either Egypt or Greece in most of these books. Certainly the origin of monotheism, the stories of Abraham, Isaac, Moses, David, Solomon, and the prophets such as Isaiah and Jeremiah are central to Western life and history, indeed to much of Islam as well. Although some of these people and topics are mentioned, they get very little emphasis. There is much more coverage of Islam than of Judaism. In addition, there is no reference at all to Jewish life and culture in the last two thousand years—until the Holocaust. In other words, the Judeo- part of the Judeo-Christian history of the West is most inadequately represented.

2. *Neglect of the Life of Jesus of Nazareth.* Whatever one thinks of Christianity, it has certainly been of central importance in world history, and the life of Jesus of Nazareth constitutes one of the more important events of that history. Indeed, many would claim his life is the most important single event in the history of the last two thousand years. Certainly the history of Europe, North and South America, and much of the Near East, Africa, and even Asia cannot be understood without reference to his life and what it has meant—for good or ill—for countless others. Yet none of these books treats the life of Jesus as anything like the important event it proved to be. A few of the books give him some coverage (e.g., Silver Burdett), but four books—Riverside, Macmillan, Laidlaw, Holt, Rinehart & Winston—give not a word of coverage to his life and teaching. Others give so little as to be banal, e.g., American Book, Allyn & Bacon, Steck-Vaughn. For example,

Steck-Vaughn gives the following as a complete summary of Jesus' life: "Jesus became a teacher. He preached that there was only One God. He told those who would listen that they must honor God by treating others with love and forgiveness." Besides the trivialization and serious omissions in this description, it has one major error. Jesus did not make a point of preaching there was "only One God"—monotheism was assumed in Jewish life, and it was hardly a focus of Jesus' message. In fact, the language "only One God" is central to Islam, not to Christianity.

To appreciate the neglect of the life of Jesus, it is only necessary to compare it with some of these same books' coverage of the life of Mohammed. In a number of texts, Mohammed's life gets much more coverage than that of Jesus. For example, consider that in Silver Burdett, the life of Jesus gets thirty-six lines, while the life of Mohammed gets 104 lines; Riverside mentions Mohammed as founder of Islam (e.g., pp. 198, 200), but Jesus is not mentioned anywhere in the text; Macmillan has a brief reference to Mohammed and his faith (p. 50) but none to Jesus. Islam gets much positive coverage in Laidlaw (for example, pp. 123-124). The rise of Islam, Islamic culture, and Mohammed himself get an eleven-page section, plus other scattered coverage. The rise of Christianity gets almost nothing (a few lines on p. 116). In these books, then, it is not that great religious figures are totally avoided—it is that Jesus is avoided.

3. *Neglect of the First One Thousand Years of Christianity.* The typical world history text studied here would cover Rome—usually noting somewhere in Roman history that Christianity spread in the period of the late Empire. The end of Rome marks the end of the section. Then the next historic period would commonly be the rise of Islam. This section is typically followed by a treatment of the feudal Middle Ages. Thus, the first one thousand years of Christianity gets very little emphasis—unlike the rise of Islam, which often gets considerable attention. Only one book, McGraw-Hill, has any significant section on the rise of Christianity or the first centuries of the church.

4. *Neglect of Eastern Orthodox Christianity and the Byzantine Empire.* With a few exceptions (e.g., McGraw-Hill, p. 126), the world of Byzantium is either not mentioned at all or is seriously neglected. This failing relates in part to the general neglect of the first one thousand years of Christian history. Only two texts have

even any modest coverage of the Eastern Orthodox world and culture—Silver Burdett and McGraw-Hill. Books without any textual reference to Eastern Orthodoxy (or Byzantium) were American Book, Steck-Vaughn, and Holt, Rinehart & Winston.

5. *Neglect of Protestantism.* One of the most obvious characteristics of many of the texts is their failure to mention the Protestant Reformation, or their tendency to give it very little emphasis. For example, American Book hardly refers to Protestantism and not at all to the Reformation; Riverside has twenty pages on Tanzania, nineteen pages on the history of the Netherlands, and sixteen pages on ancient Crete, but it makes no reference to Martin Luther or Calvin, and there is almost nothing on Protestantism. The absence of reference to Protestantism in Holland is particularly noteworthy given that country's history. (One commentator on this study noted that a historical treatment "of the Netherlands with no reference to John Calvin or the Reformation ... is roughly equivalent to summarizing the history of the United States without mentioning George Washington or the American Revolution."

Silver Burdett's text, although it generally provides one of the relatively better treatments of religion, hardly mentions the Reformation. Holt, Rinehart & Winston and Steck-Vaughn have nothing on the Reformation, but their orientation is more on world cultures than world history. Even the texts that do include the Reformation usually do not discuss the theological differences that were at stake. Religious differences—the fundamental basis of the conflict—are typically omitted. For example, Scott, Foresman (p. 270) mentions Martin Luther and the break from the Catholic church, but no reason for the break is mentioned. Only McGraw-Hill and, in a minor way, Allyn & Bacon refer to plausible religious reasons for the Reformation. This neglect of Protestantism further supports the thesis that there is some kind of repression or denial of Christianity (especially Protestantism) in these texts.

6. *Neglect of Christianity in the Modern World.* None of these texts gives much emphasis at all to Christianity as a living cultural and historical force in the world of today or in the last two hundred years, especially in the United States. Like good social anthropologists, the writers of these books *do* give religion a significant place in the life of many other cultures today. For

example, the Arab world is never described without a serious treatment of Islam; likewise many other foreign cultures or countries are described as having important religious components. At times some religious aspects of such places as today's France (e.g., Scott, Foresman, pp. 69-71) or Italy (e.g., Scott Foresman, pp. 138, 158-160) or of the conflict in northern Ireland (McGraw-Hill, Laidlaw) are mentioned. Often South America is discussed as having important Catholic aspects to its society. (As already noted, such an awareness of religion in the United States is not recognized in grades 1-5.)

In addition to the points mentioned above, a feminist emphasis, even projected anachronistically into the distant past, is present in some texts. The relatively small number of women of influence in the past are mentioned, even featured, out of proportion to their historical significance. For example, Anne Hutchinson is almost always misrepresented in a way that is proto-feminist; Laidlaw mentions that Muslims kept women out of power (p. 186) and then features the one known sultunate of a Muslim woman (it lasted four years). A particularly offensive example of this is the Laidlaw treatment of Joan of Arc (pp. 256-257). Her story is told without any reference at all to God, to religion, or to her being a saint. The treatment is entirely secular and seems to have been included simply because Joan of Arc was a woman.

Study Four: Family Values in Social Studies Textbooks— Grades 1-4

This project addressed how family and family values are treated in social studies texts.

Sample and Scoring. This study involved only the books for grades 1-4—books purporting to introduce the child to an understanding of contemporary American society. As previously noted, the grade 5 and 6 texts addressed American history and world history and culture. These books were excluded as irrelevant to the issue of family values because family life in America was not referred to in any way.

Each page of the grade 1-4 books was read, and any reference to a family, to family life, or to someone identified as a member of family, e.g., father, mother, or aunt, was scored as a "family" emphasis. Those books that had only zero-five pages referring to family were judged to have "slight" emphasis on the family. If there were six to fifteen family pages, the book was judged to have "moderate" family emphasis; sixteen to twenty-five family pages was scored as a "strong" family emphasis, and more than twenty-five pages as a "very strong" family emphasis.

In addition, certain key family concepts and words were looked for in the texts and were scored as present or absent for a given book.

Results. 1. *Amount of Family Emphasis.* The books vary greatly among grades and publishers in their emphasis on family (see Table D-3, Appendix D). For example, the grade 4 texts often have no representation of family life at all because of their focus on geography. Grades 1-3 usually have some family emphasis and often have a marked emphasis on family. To summarize, we found that in each publisher's set of four books, there is at least one book with a moderate—that is, six to fifteen pages—family emphasis. The Steck-Vaughn books have an especially heavy family emphasis; all of its books were rated "strong" or "very strong" on family. Many other publishers are generally pretty strong on family as well—although Riverside and Laidlaw are weak on the family. However, in terms of amount of family emphasis, most of these sets do well.

2. *Kind of Family Emphasis.* But serious issues arise when one looks at the *kind* of family emphasis—when one moves from quantity to quality. For example, when an explicit definition of the family is given, it is seriously deficient or disturbing. For example, Laidlaw (grade 2, p. 6) states merely "a family is a group of people." Such a definition is so obviously vague and inaccurate that no further comment seems necessary. The teacher's edition of this book elaborates on the definition so as to make a family a group of people "who identify themselves as family members." Thus there is only a subjective definition of a family. This notion characterizes *all* these books, not just Laidlaw.

Commonly a family is defined as "the people you live with" (e.g., Silver Burdett, grade 1, p. 18). The entire emphasis in these books is on the many types of family—all implicitly equally legitimate.

Typically, however, no explicit, objective definition of family is given; instead an implicit, subjective definition is provided by the pictures and stories referring to family life. In these cases, the definition provided by the images is that a family consists of those people, whoever they might be, that the child lives with. Families are often shown without a father, sometimes without a mother, and sometimes as a couple without children.

Still more importantly, basic ideas with respect to the nature of family are entirely excluded from these texts. There is not one text reference to marriage as the foundation of the family. Indeed not even the word marriage or wedding occurs once in the forty books! The possible one exception to this could be the Scott, Foresman (grade 2, p. 131) reference to a neighbor's wedding, but this occurs in a short treatment of life in Spain! (Apparently some people do still get married in that old-fashioned country.) Further, it is relevant to note that neither the word husband nor wife occurs once in any of these books. It is clear that marriage is not seen as having any relevance, much less a central one, to the definition of family. Educators may constantly bemoan teenage pregnancy and the frequency of illegitimate children, but their own textbooks begin fostering the notion of family without marriage in grades 1 to 4.

Other basic family values are also noticeable by their absence. Not one of the many families described in these books features a homemaker—that is, referred to a woman principally dedicated to acting as a wife and mother—as a model. Indeed, only one or two stories in all the books showed in picture or in some other indirect way that a woman was probably a homemaker. The words *housewife* and *homemaker* never occur in these books. Yet there are countless references to mothers and other women working outside of the home in occupations such as medicine, transportation, and politics. There is not one citation indicating that the occupation of a mother or housewife represents an important job, one with integrity, one that provides real satisfactions. There is one story in which the woman presumably *is* a mother and housewife—but this fact isn't noted or featured in any way. Closely related to this is the absence of traditional family sex roles. Such roles are occasionally represented when family life in the historic past is described or when families in other countries are featured. However, there is not one portrayal of a contemporary American family that clearly features traditional sex roles.

Study Five: Other Observations on Social Studies Textbooks— Grades 1-4

In the course of the reading of these books, certain interesting observations were made that had not been anticipated. They are summarized below.

A Strong Partisan Political Emphasis. Most of these books single out certain prominent people for special emphasis. These people are not necessary for the discussion of social life or the history of the United States (such as presidents would be) but are considered by the authors to be important people who would interest the students. Such people are selected to serve as role models for the students since they are usually featured under such headings as "Famous People," or "Someone You Should Know," or "People Who Made a Difference." People whose major contributions have occurred since World War II are specifically noted as contemporary political role models. In this study, a person was scored as a political role model if he or she is singled out for distinctive biographical treatment and if the person was active in political life or well known for his or her political or ideological significance, e.g., Martin Luther King, Jr. The person had to have a picture, and had to be given a paragraph or page of special treatment separate from any history that might be under discussion at the time. Because we asked the question, "Is there *political* and *ideological* bias in these books?," people selected as role models from the arts, sports, and the world of science are not included in this analysis. But some liberal bias was noted even in these fields, for example, in the selection of such artists as Woodie Guthrie, Leonard Bernstein, Beverly Sills, and others.

The characteristics of those noted in Table 5 make clear the implicit political agenda of these books. It is even hard to find any Republican role models—the exceptions being Milicent Fenwick, a liberal, pro-abortion, pro-ERA congresswoman;

Table 5

All People of Post-World War II Political and Social Significance Selected for Special Biographical Emphasis (Role Models) in the Social Studies Texts: Grades 1-6. (See text for details of selection.)

Name	Party	Accomplishment	Publisher; Grade
Herman Badillo	Dem	N.Y. City politician	Holt-4
Romana Banuelos	Dem	Treasurer of U.S.	Laidlaw-1
Thomas Bradley (2 times)	Dem	Mayor, Los Angeles	Holt-4 McGraw-Hill-3
Ralph Bunche	Dem	United Nations Office	Amer-4
Rachel Carson (2 times)	N.A	Ecology movement	Holt-1 Amer-4
Raul Castro	Dem	Governor of Arizona	Laidlaw-5
Henry Cisneros	Dem	Mayor, San Antonio	Scott, Fores.-4
Vine DeLoria	N.A.	American Indian rights	Laidlaw-1
Millicent Fenwick	Rep	U.S. Congress, N.J.	Allyn & Bacon-4
Ella Grasso	Dem	Governor of Connecticut	Scott, Fores.-4
Patricia Harris	Dem	Lawyer; black rights	Holt-4
Dolores Huerta	N.A.	United Farm Workers	Scott, Fores.-3
Nancy Kassebaum	Rep	U.S. Senate, Kansas	Laidlaw-2
Maggie Kuhn	N.A.	Gray Panthers/ Feminist	Amer-4
Martin L. King, Jr. (3 times)	N.A.	Civil Rts. leader	Laidlaw-1, Holt-4, Silver Burdett-4
Clare Booth Luce	Rep	Ambassador	Laidlaw-1
Thurgood Marshall	N.A.	Supreme Court Justice	Laidlaw-2
Margaret Mead (2 times)	N.A.	Anthropologist	Holt-6 Amer-4
Patsy Mink	Dem	U.S. Congress, Hawaii	Holt-4
Julian Nava	Dem	Ambass. to Mex; author	Amer-4
Dixie Lee Ray	Dem	Gov. of Washington	Amer-4
Eleanor Roosevelt (3 times)	Dem	Founder of U.N.; various good works	Holt-4, Scholas-6 Scott, Fores.-4
Coleman Young	Dem	Mayor, Detroit	Scott, Fores.-3

Nancy Kassebaum, a moderate Republican; and Clare Booth Luce, a conservative Republican and an ambassador who was active thirty years ago. A reader would think there are no male Republicans in the country, much less any active conservatives, male or female, of any political stripe during the last twenty years. What is also striking is that many of the people chosen are active in politics now—or were when the books were published. In short, there is a clear political character of a partisan, liberal bent to these social studies texts.

There are various ways to document the substantial liberal political bias of these selections. Examples of people never selected are Douglas MacArthur, Robert A. Taft, Barry Goldwater, William Buckley, Jesse Helms, Jack Kemp; no neo-conservatives are mentioned, e.g., Irving Kristol; not one of the youthful breed of business entrepreneurs behind today's high tech business (Silicon Valley, for example) is ever featured; indeed not a businessman (or woman) active since World War II was selected as a role model. Such women as Nellie Gray, Phyllis Schlafly, or Jeanne Kirkpatrick are never represented. And, of course, Billy Graham, Oral Roberts, Fulton Sheen, Pat Robertson, Jerry Falwell, and even Norman Vincent Peale are omitted. (None of those people were even mentioned elsewhere in these books even in passing, much less as a role model.)

Political bias also shows in the reliable tendency of these books to characterize recent (and much of past) American history in terms of three issues or themes: minority rights, feminism, and ecological and environmental issues. In every case, the *pro* position is presented as positive; the opposition is never given any serious treatment. There are no conservative positions identified or supported in any way in any of these books. For example, there is simply no mention of the anti-ERA movement, the pro-life movement, or opposition to affirmative action, or the tax revolt. The idea that government might be too big, too controlling, is never mentioned.

Here is a typical example of how feminism is represented in an implicit manner: Consider pages 98-99 of American Book, grade 1. These pages consist only of large photographs of representative people working. The pictures primarily represent role reversal. In the teacher's edition, the teacher is instructed to comment to students on the pictures as follows: "Teacher asks: How many of the workers on these pages can you identify?" (The workers on p. 98 include women working in the oil industry, a male telephone operator, and a woman doctor. Those on p. 99 include a woman auto mechanic, a clown, and two male researchers.)

Figure 3:2

"EAT YOUR DINNER, ARTHUR. DON'T YOU WANT TO GROW UP TO BE BIG AND STRONG LIKE YOUR MOTHER?"

Some typical pages from Riverside (grade 2), one of the most obviously feminist set of texts, include depictions of a woman mayor (p. 73), a woman construction worker (p. 74), a woman police officer (p. 76), a woman firefighter (p. 77), a woman supervisor (p. 77), a woman judge (p. 79), and a woman mail carrier (p. 79).

Although Riverside and American Book are probably the most aggressive in portrayals of sex role reversals, all forty books have a unisex emphasis. Not one of these books presents in any form a sympathetic portrayal of traditional sex role models for the contemporary United States.

Neglect of Business and Free Enterprise

The basic concepts and the common experience of free enterprise is not represented in any of these books. Of course, such ideas as supporting big business or corporate capitalism, aside from their controversial character, are abstract and hard to grasp for children in grade school. But the easily understood notion that many people start a business and work hard for its success is simply without representation in these books. For example, there are millions of family businesses in this country. Thousands of such small enterprises are started every day by people of all social classes and ethnic groups. Indeed, family-oriented businesses, either full- or part-time, are especially characteristic of many new immigrants and blue collar families. Nor is there one presentation of the importance of saving money, or of having a savings account.

A family business, for example, would make an appropriate setting for introducing children to their neighborhoods, to the nature of economic transaction, and to community structure and civic life—yet none of these books present these concepts through this vehicle. As a result of such silences, these books completely fail to portray one of the central parts of the American dream and the American reality: that of becoming financially successful by going into business for oneself.

A Money and Career Emphasis. All of these text sequences present work as having two—and only two—primary meanings. One is to be paid money and then to use the money to buy goods to satisfy needs and wants. A typical treatment shows a man or woman—explicitly or implicitly the father or mother—working at a job, being paid, and then going to the store to buy something. That is, these books seem especially concerned with portraying economic life as the consumption of material goods, thus ensuring another generation of docile consumers.

The other meaning given to work is that it gives status—as in a career. Although this is not mentioned in the text, the images often convey the idea that work is a relatively pleasing or satisfactory activity in its own right. It is certainly not presented as drudgery.

Neglect of Charity and Good Works. However, there is not one mention in the texts of the fact that many people don't work for money, e.g., homemakers; or that many people volunteer their services to hospitals and other organizations; or that many people exchange goods and services (barter); or that many people, presumably many school teachers, work in part for rewards other than money. No text mentioned regular work performed out of concern for others or undertaken because of the intrinsic value of certain kinds of work. *The absence of any concern for non-material values is so extreme that not one book's discussion of a family budget includes any money for charity or for others in need.* Giving money to a church is never mentioned. Instead, the primary emphasis is on personal enjoyment, status, and the consumer economy. By implication, the message is clear that if you work and aren't paid money, you—and what you do—don't really count.

FOUR

Religion in High School American History

THIS STUDY, NUMBER FOUR, investigates how religion is represented in American history textbooks used throughout the country in the eleventh or twelfth grade. These books normally present an extensive yearlong concentration on American history.

The Sample. California does not provide a high school American history adoption list; Texas has an adoption list of only five books, and one of the books on this list appears to have been adopted only by Texas and no other state (Rand McNally). Therefore, the following basis for selecting the history textbooks was used.

From the fourteen states that provided adoption lists for this study, there were twelve textbooks adopted by five or more states. These books were judged as representative. From this list of twelve, eight texts were selected at random. These eight are shown in Table 6. This list included the two books most widely adopted, namely the Harcourt Brace Jovanovich text adopted by twelve of the fourteen adoption states and the Holt, Rinehart & Winston text selected by eleven of the adoption states. The eight books in the sample are highly representative: on the average they account for 60% of those texts on the adoption lists of the states that provided EPIE an adoption list. A conservative estimate is that 50% of the country's students taking American history use one of the books in the sample.

Table 6

The High School History Texts (Grade 11 or 12)
Used in the Sample for Study Four

Publisher and Copyright Date	Authors	Title	Adoption States*
1. Addison Wesley 1979 (3rd ed.)	R. Madgic S. Seaburg F. Stopsky R. Winks	*The American Experience*	AL, FL, GA, IN, NM, OK, SC, TX, VA
2. Globe 1984	S. Schwartz J. O'Connor	*Exploring Our Nation's History*	AL, FL, GA, NV, NM
3. Harcourt Brace Jovanovich 1982	L. Todd M. Curti	*Rise of the American Nation*	AL, FL, GA, IN, MS, NV, NM, NC, OK, TX, UT, VA
4. Holt, Rinehart & Winston 1982	N. Risjord T. Haywoode	*People and Our Country*	AL, FL, GA, ID, IN, MS, NV, NM, OK, SC, TX
5. Houghton Mifflin 1981	J. Shenton J. Benson R. Jakoubek	*These United States*	AL, GA, ID, IN, NV, NM, OK, VA
6. Laidlaw (2nd ed.) 1981	G. Linden E. Wassenich D. Brink W. Jones, Jr.	*A History of Our American Republic*	AL, FL, ID, IN, NM, OK, SC, TX, VA
7. Macmillan 1981	H. Bragdon S. McCutchen	*History of a Free People*	AL, GA, ID, MS, NM, OK, SC, UT, VA
8. Silver Burdett 1983 Vol 1 and 2	J. Bass G. Billias E. Lapsansky	*America and the Americans*	AL, FL, GA, ID, NM, NC, UT, VA

*Adoption lists provided by EPIE; note many states do not have official adoption lists. See text for evidence of the national representativeness of the texts.

Scoring. Each page of each history book was read and references to religion were noted. In addition, since each text has at least a moderately thorough index, all index entries relating to religion were checked. All of the scoring for each book was independently verified by an outside scorer supplied by EPIE. About 10% of the references to religion were missed by the author, but picked up by the EPIE scorer. These additional references were used when arriving at the general summaries described below. The summaries were also evaluated for accuracy by an EPIE scorer. Although an occasional reference to religion may have been missed, it is unlikely that any important treatment was overlooked. the protocols (summary of the scoring for each text) are in Appendix C of the ERIC report.

General Description. On average, these books are twice as long as the fifth grade texts, running to seven hundred or eight hundred pages; they also have more words per page, fewer photos, and fewer exercises. As a consequence, these books had at least three or four times more coverage of American history than the fifth grade social studies books. They are written in a much more scholarly style and some of the authors are quite prominent American historians. For example, consider *Rise of the American Nation* (Todd and Curti. New York: Harcourt Brace Jovanovich, 1982) which has gone through several editions. Curti is listed as the Fredrick Jackson Turner Professor of American History (now Emeritus) at the University of Wisconsin and is a past president of the American Historical Association. Dr. Todd is a prominent educationist active in the professional world of social studies.

Norman K. Risjord, senior author of *People and Our Country* (N.Y.: Holt, Rinehart & Winston, 1982), is a professor of history at the University of Wisconsin; Robin W. Winks, fourth author of *The American Experience,* 3rd ed. (1979), is professor of history at Yale University. The three authors of *America and Americans,* Herbert J. Bass, George A. Billias, and Emma Jones Lapsansky, are professors of history at Temple University, Clark University, and Temple University respectively.

The other authors of these books are either professors of education or well-known educationists. In other words, these books are not only much more substantial than the grade 5 social studies texts, but the authors presumably represent a much higher level of competence—and indeed in a few cases they represent the very highest level of historical scholarship as practiced in the country.

However, the fact that these books have clearly identified authors does not necessarily mean that these books are actually written by them. In some cases, the authors might have written the first edition, but after years of subsequent revisions by the publishers' own editors and writers, there is often little left that can be honestly attributed to the supposed authors. The most accurate description of the process of writing a textbook I have found is given by Frances FitzGerald in her book on American history texts (1979). She points out that it is not unusual for one of the prominent historian authors to have died before many of the events occurred which are presumably described by them in the text. Because of the excessive amount of in-house editing and changing, FitzGerald dryly comments: "Texts are not 'written' anymore; they are as the people in the industry say, 'developed,' and this process involves large numbers of people and many compromises." She also notes that the lower the grade level, the larger the number of editors and advisers involved in "developing" the book.

In any case, we should expect a great deal more of high school American history texts than of the grade 5 social studies books.

Results

Book Summaries. A summary of each book provides the clearest picture of its own particular weaknesses and strengths. The important failures that all these texts share are noted in the conclusions section. The texts are listed by publisher in alphabetical order as in Table 6.

1. Addison-Wesley, *The American Experience* (1979), Madgic, Seaburg, Stopsky, and Winks. This book begins with a surprisingly good section on the Puritan heritage—at times somewhat controversial, but that is surely inevitable. The authors also do well on the religious roots of the abolitionists, Catholic mitigation of slavery in South America, religion in the nineteenth century, and the Social Gospel movement; and they provide some

treatment of religious themes up until the 1920s or so. For the last fifty years, however, religion almost disappears. For example, the religious origins and aspects of Martin Luther King, Jr. are treated as almost nonexistent.

The authors cover Protestant fundamentalism only with reference to the Scopes Trial of 1925. The treatment is critical but not unrealistic. The bias comes from the fact that they do not present any other aspects of conservative Protestantism.

Also, the authors have nothing on the urban religious revivals of the 1870s and 1880s; nothing on the Holiness-Pentecostal movement; and there is nothing on American Catholicism in the nineteenth and twentieth centuries except references to prejudice against it.

2. Globe, *Exploring Our Nation's History* (1984), Schwartz and O'Connor. This book's coverage of religion in the eighteenth and nineteenth centuries is extremely weak. For example, there is no reference to the Great Awakening of the 1740s, none to the Salem Witch Trials or to the Second Great Awakening of the 1830s and 1840s; no reference to the Mormons.

Except for the issue of religious toleration, this book shows little concern with religion in the Colonial Period. It so seriously fails to capture the importance of religion not only in the Colonial Period but also for the Abolitionist and Civil War Period that—to put it charitably—the book is a misrepresentation of American history.

Coverage of the last one hundred years is better, although here it is primarily liberal issues as related to religion that are emphasized. The authors mention significant aspects of church support for the humanitarian reforms of 1880-1910 and the presence of ministers in the progressive movement. They note the KKK as motivated by religious as well as racial bigotry; they note anti-Catholic bias in the election of J.F. Kennedy; and they point out, as many texts do not, that Martin Luther King, Jr. based his ideas on Christian and democratic ideals.

However, there is no reference to the urban religious revivals of the 1870s and 1880s, the Holiness and Pentecostal movement, the fundamentalists, the Bible Belt, the Born-Again movement, or to figures such as Billy Graham.

At the end of the book's eight units, the authors list eighty-three important dates in American history. Only one is religious—the first Thanksgiving in 1621. Apparently, there have been no events related to religion of any historical importance since 1621!

3. Harcourt Brace Jovanovich, *Rise of the American Nation* (1982), Todd and Curti. In many respects this book's treatment of religion is seriously inadequate. Specifically, there is no reference to any of the following: the great revival, sometimes called the Second Great Awakening, of the 1830s and 1840s; the Holiness or Pentecostal movement of 1880-1910; the world of fundamentalist or of conservative Protestantism, e.g., the Bible Belt; the Born-Again and Jesus movements of the 1960s and 1970s; the Social Gospel movement, e.g., Rauschenbusch, circa 1900; or to liberal Protestantism as a cultural or political force in this century. Martin Luther King, Jr.'s religious connection and some of his religious support are noted. The Black Muslims are mentioned very briefly. Except for these last two references, there is no reference to religion in America in the twentieth century.

Expressive of this omission of religion is the list called "Chronology of Events in American History" at the end of the book. This list contains over 450 events considered important in

Figure 4:1

" YOU MAY WRITE A REPORT ON ANY INSECT YOU'D LIKE ... EXCEPT, OF COURSE, THE PRAYING MANTIS ! "

American history. The only three events referring to religion are (1) the landing of the Pilgrims in 1620; (2) the adoption of the Toleration Act in Maryland in 1649; and (3) the settling of the Mormons at Salt Lake in 1847. Other events included as more historic and important than *any* aspect of religion in the last 130 years include the first State Minimum Wage Act enacted in 1912; the creation of the Veteran's Bureau in 1921; the establishment of the Securities Exchange Commission in 1934; and the establishment of the Department of Transportation in 1966. This book has sections on changes in American economic life, important events in our cultural history, and changes and developments in science and technology—but religion is never identified as important. With respect to religion, a major aspect of American life, this text, coauthored by a past president of the American Historical Society, offers a serious distortion of the historical record.

4. Holt, Rinehart & Winston, *People and Our Country* (1982), Risjord and Haywoode. This book mentions most of the standard religious events but generally quite briefly. Reference is made to both Great Awakenings; Jonathan Edwards, George Whitefield, and Cotton Mather; Mormons; Christian Science; the Social Gospel; Dwight Moody (the only book to mention this important figure of the urban religious revivals); Rauschenbusch; progressive religion; Seventh Day Adventists; religious aspects of Martin Luther King, Jr.; and nineteenth and twentieth century anti-Catholic prejudice. The book also notes such important Catholic figures as Elizabeth Seton, Isaac Hecker, and Mother Cabrini. Further, the text mentions Jewish immigration in 1890 and American anti-Semitism.

However, there is no reference made to the Holiness and Pentecostal movement (though, as noted, this book does give a paragraph to Dwight Moody and urban revivalism—a part of the Holiness movement); there is no reference to fundamentalism, the Bible Belt, or the Born-Again movement.

Putting aside the topic of religion, let us note that unfortunately this book ends with a very partisan treatment of recent history. Specifically, from 1945 to the present (i.e., chapters twenty-eight to thirty-four), the book features the following people in a special section called *Sidenote to History*. (This section is very like the presentation of role models in the social studies texts.) Here is the list of the people who are featured: (1) Perle Mesta (feminist and woman ambassador); (2) Ralph Bunche (U.N. mediator, Nobel Peace Prize); (3) Jackie Robinson (baseball player breaking the color barrier); (4) Chief Justice Earl Warren (Warren Court); (5) Julius Robert Oppenheimer (opposition to building the nuclear bomb); (6) Martin Luther King, Jr. ("I have a dream"); (7) Cesar Chavez ("La Causa" and the grape pickers strike); and (8) Ralph Nader (public defender); in short, a list that might have come straight from the editorial pages of the *New York Times, Washington Post,* or *Boston Globe.*

5. Houghton Mifflin, *These United States* (1981), Shenton, Benson, and Jakoubek. This book mentions the Salem Witch Trials, the First Great Awakening, Jonathan Edwards, and George Whitefield and gives the best coverage of any text (three pages) on the revivals and great religious changes circa 1840. The authors even note the religious freedom rationale for the founding of Catholic schools. This is the only one of the eight history texts to do so. The authors mention the Social Gospel around 1890-1910, the presence of the church at the center of black American life, and the religious motivation of Martin Luther King, Jr.

However, this book fails to mention the urban revivals and the Holiness-Pentecostal movement of 1880-1910. It is totally silent on the Bible Belt and fundamentalist Protestantism.

Although its coverage of topics is better than most of the books, the overall effect is disappointing—as in its list of over three hundred important dates in American history. This list has only three religious events: the 1630 Puritan settlement of Boston; the 1692 Witchcraft Trials in Massachusetts; and the 1775 Quakers' founding of the first American antislavery society. These are the only three religion-connected events given— nothing else for the next 205 years (the list ends in 1980). Events after 1775 that are considered more important than any event related to religion: in 1816, the second United States Bank was chartered; in 1878, California ceased to be bilingual; in 1887, electric street cars were introduced in Richmond, Virginia; and in 1917, literacy for immigrants was adopted.

6. Laidlaw, *A History of Our American People* (1981), Linden, Wassenich, Brink, and Jones. This book is really quite weak in its coverage of religion. For example, it has no reference to the First Great Awakening (c. 1740) and no reference to the Salem Witch Trials. It does refer to the revivals of 1820-1840. Its treatment of religion in the Colonial Period is standard but thin; it refers to the religious freedom issue through mention of the Quakers as a "religious group" which was involved in the Abolitionist movement. There is no serious discussion of the Christian role in fostering the antislave sentiment prior to the Civil War.

The text has a slightly better religious coverage starting in the mid-nineteenth century. The authors discuss the Mormons in some detail and refer to the Social Gospel movement, Rauschenbusch, and religious involvement in progressivism. However, there is no reference to the urban religious revivals or to the Holiness or Pentecostal movements, nor any reference to Catholic schools or hospitals, much less to Catholic or recent Protestant schools as expressions of freedom of religion.

In the twentieth century coverage, the KKK is mentioned as anti-Jewish and anti-Catholic; and reference is made to the J.F. Kennedy Catholic election issue. Martin Luther King, Jr.'s life is linked to Christianity.

Some of the special religious problems with this text are

1. Fundamentalism (p. 532) is *defined* as made up of rural people who "follow the values or traditions of an earlier period"—without any reference to religion.

2. There is a systematic lack of religious emphasis. Specifically, throughout the book important dates, starting with 1607, are noted under the following topics: economic, social, political, and work and leisure. Of 642 listed events, only six refer to religion: (1) 1649—Religious Toleration Act in Maryland; (2) 1661—first Bible published in America; (3) 1692—Salem Witch Trials; (4) 1769—Spanish missions in California; (5) religious revivals of 1858 (sic); and (6) 1875—Hebrew Union College founded in Cincinnati. (This is a Reform Jewish College, i.e., liberal Judaism.)

This list has nothing on religion since 1875. There is no mention of a Conservative or Orthodox Jewish institution, of such Catholic universities as Georgetown or Notre Dame, or about the many Bible colleges, such as Nyack College, one of the first such institutions.

The following supposedly important dates in American history are listed in this book: 1893, Yale introduces ice hockey; 1897, first subway completed in Boston; 1920, United States wins first place in Olympic Games; 1930, Irish Sweepstakes becomes popular; 1960, Pittsburgh Pirates win World Series; 1962, Twist—a popular dance craze. The above categories make it clear that such trivia is given more emphasis than any aspect of religion in the last one hundred years.

3. Religion in the twentieth century is rarely mentioned.

This book also shows a strong feminist leaning. For example, there are nineteen feminist dates listed in the list of important American dates—thus it could be inferred that feminism throughout American history is considered more than three times as important as religion—and over the last one hundred years or so, feminism is portrayed as ten or twenty times more important than religion. One example of pro-feminist bias is the fact that page 642 lists Senate approval in 1972 of the ERA under the heading "Social Progress." This is not to suggest that feminism is not a legitimate and important part of American history; it is to suggest that the proportional emphasis is distorted, especially over the last fifty to one hundred years.

This book also includes fairly large coverage of the beatniks, the youth culture, the counter-culture, and the new left. However, it has nothing on the Jesus movement, the Born-Again movement, or the emergence of the religious right.

7. Macmillan, *History of a Free People* (1981), Bragdon and McCutchen. In general, this book offers an average, though still far from adequate, treatment of religion in American history. For example, there is no mention of the First Great Awakening as important to American history. There is no mention of Jonathan Edwards, the Mathers, the Wesleys, or the Salem Witch Trials.

In their treatment of the nineteenth century, Bragdon and McCutchen mention the important religious movements associated with the Second Great Awakening, and they give some coverage to the Social Gospel, liberal Protestantism, and progressivism in the early twentieth century. However, they have nothing on the urban revivals of the 1870s and 1880s or on the great Holiness-Pentecostal movements (1880-1910); nothing on fundamentalism, e.g., the Bible-Belt, the Scopes Trial, or the Born-Again movement of the 1960s and 1970s.

At the end of each chapter there is a section presenting a list of names and events headed "Who, What and Why Important." The book's thirty-four chapter lists have 814 items. At most, thirteen have a connection to religion—i.e., less than 2%—and only four or five of these come after the Civil War. Most of the "religious events," such as Anne Hutchinson and Roger Williams and the Maryland Toleration Act, are really references to religious freedom and toleration and not to religion per se.

8. Silver Burdett, *America and Americans* (1983), Bass, Billias, and Lapsansky. *Vol. 1. Colonial Period to Reconstruction.* There is a moderate emphasis on religion in the early Colonial Period, such as the Puritans, dissenters, e.g., Hutchinson, and Williams (p. 25, cf.); but there is no reference to the Salem Witch Trials. The text moves on to the Maryland Toleration Act (and Catholics); Quakers; the Pennsylvania story; religious aspects of colonial government, and the diversity of religions in the United States. Then it mentions the Great Awakening of 1730-40. There is no reference to Jonathan Edwards, Cotton Mather, or the Wesleys. George Whitefield is noted in connection with Phillis Wheatley, a religious Colonial black poetess. Religious origins of or links to the Abolitionist movement are noted, especially with respect to the Quakers. The Whitmans (Narcissa and Marcus) are given a short paragraph as missionaries to the Oregon country. The Mormons are given a full page; it is noted that slaves turned to religion. There is no reference to the Second Great Awakening.

Vol. 2. From Reconstruction to Present. The index has no entry for religion or for specific religious denominations. There is really little reference to religion as a social force in twentieth century America. The book does have a short section on the Scopes Trial; a short reference to the Women's Christian Temperance Union (WCTU); a reference to the anti-Semitic, anti-Catholic prejudice of the KKK; and a reference to the anti-Catholic bias in politics as reflected in the presidential campaigns of Al Smith (1928) and John F. Kennedy (1960).

This serious lack of treatment of religion in the twentieth century is to some extent relieved by the relatively frequent mention of religion in biographical material. Here it is presented as a force in the lives of President Wilson, President Eisenhower, and Martin Luther King, Jr.

Again, political liberalism is the main position of the book in its coverage of the last forty years. For example, the "Great Americans" featured to represent the United States—and to function as role models—since 1945 are Martin Luther King, Jr., Rachel Carson, John F. Kennedy, Margaret Mead, Thurgood Marshall, and Walt Disney. (Only Walt Disney is not a standard hero of the political left; he seems to be a middle-of-the-road figure, with little political significance one way or the other.) Each person gets from four to six full pages of biographical treatment.

History Textbooks: Conclusions

With respect to the treatment of religion, a number of important traits characterize all these history books. First, not one of these texts acknowledges, much less emphasizes, the great religious energy and creativity of the United States.

Alexis de Tocqueville, long recognized as an important and astute foreign observer of the United States, wrote in the 1840s after his visit to this country:

> The religious atmosphere of the country was the first thing that struck me on arrival in the United States. The longer I stayed in the country, the more conscious I became of the important political consequences resulting from this novel situation.
>
> Religion, which never intervenes directly in the government of American society, should therefore be considered as the first of their political institutions. . . .[1]

This understanding of America so powerfully described by Tocqueville, and so widely accepted by scholars of American society, is completely without representation in these history texts.

For all practical purposes, religion is hardly mentioned as existing in America in the last seventy-five to one hundred years;

in particular, none of these books includes any serious coverage of conservative Protestantism in this century, although a few books mentioned the Scopes Trial. That this is the topic chosen to represent conservative Protestantism could be seen as a sign of liberal bias itself. There is not one book that recognizes the continuity of the revival and evangelical movements throughout American history since the Colonial Period. Such religious movements continue today and have much in common with today's religious right. But a student curious about the origin and history of the religious right will find no information in these books.

There are still other major criticisms to be made of these books. None of them offers any serious appreciation of positive Catholic contributions to American life. Prejudice against Catholics is commonly noted, but positive contributions in terms of the assimilation of countless immigrants, the many hospitals and orphanages built by Catholics, and the significance of the Catholic school system are (with one exception) not mentioned. Likewise, the very many positive contributions of American Jews receive almost no notice.

Even the standard religious aspects or events of American history are often omitted from these books. For example, many fail to mention one (or both) of the Great Awakenings, or the Salem Witch Trials, or the deep links between various Christian denominations and the antislavery movement, or the basic Christian character of Martin Luther King, Jr.'s life and movement. One indication of the biased treatment of religion in American history is the universal tendency to omit from the lists of important historical events almost all dates referring to religion, especially in the last one hundred years.

An additional characteristic of these texts is their common tendency to omit conservative political issues and conservative historical figures in presenting American history since World War II.

Robert Bryan's Report

Before concluding this section on American history textbooks, I would like to summarize and comment on a report by Robert

Bryan.[2] This recently published report consists of a review of American history textbooks approved for use in the Montgomery County, Maryland, school system—a school system in suburban Washington, D.C., highly respected throughout the nation. I have chosen to focus on Bryan's study because he specifically investigates how religion is treated in American high school history books and because Maryland is not one of the states that contributed to the textbook adoption list for my investigation. More importantly, I am introducing some of Bryan's results and conclusions because he is a trained historian (Ph.D. in church history from the University of London) who has focused on many of the more important historical and philosophic issues raised by the treatment of religion in our high school history books. The present (NIE) study has focused almost entirely on what is *not* in these books, on the books' enormous blind spots. Equally important but more complex is the question of how these texts do interpret religion when it is presented. For example, all these books mention the Puritans in seventeenth century New England. But Bryan examines just how the Puritans are represented, as well as many other issues.

Bryan evaluated the twenty American history books approved for use in the Montgomery County Public School system; five of the eight texts evaluated here were also on Bryan's list of twenty. Thus, Bryan's sample overlaps appreciably with the present study but also involves fifteen additional texts. The five books in common are those published by Globe; Harcourt Brace Jovanovich; Holt, Rinehart & Winston; Laidlaw; and Macmillan (see Table 6).

Bryan notes the importance of American history for high school students by pointing out that it is the only discipline in which students can actually make contact with scholarship. That is, math and science at the high school level primarily involve the learning of skills. English literature involves reading books, but usually this means the original story and not the tradition of literary interpretation and criticism. It is, as Bryan notes, in the study of history that students should encounter scholarship and reasoning. And it is here, in history, that the student should make serious contact with the primary goals of education. According to the Montgomery County school board, a primary goal of high school education is to acquaint the student with his or her "legal, moral, ethical, and cultural heritage."[3] It seems safe to assume that religion is central to this moral and cultural heritage. After all, "[r]eligion, whatever it happens to be, is always fundamental to the institutions of society... its influence is always pervasive... a work is not historical... if it fails to place the past in the context of its fundamental beliefs."[4]

After going over these twenty books Bryan concluded:

There is remarkable consensus to the effect that, after 1700, Christianity has no historical presence in America. . . . *These textbooks are written to propound the thesis that America was settled for the sake of religious freedom, and that religious freedom means the absence of religion* [emphasis in original].... Once the [early Eastern seaboard] settlement has been effected, and the population has escaped from the trammels of religion, religion need not be mentioned again. There are exceptions to this general rule, but they are so sporadic as to be incapable of conveying anything like the true importance of religion in America. . . .[5]

It is clear that Montgomery County's goal of acquainting the student with his or her "moral, ethical, and cultural heritage" is far from being met.

Bryan identifies many important religious aspects of the first one hundred years of our country that are of central importance—yet which are not mentioned. For example, Bryan notes that:

The books state generally that one of the chief reasons for emigration to the New World was freedom to worship as one pleased. And of course, this is true, within limits. Asserting it and reasserting it without qualification and without explanation—particularly without explanation of the specifically Christian aspects of the settlement in every colony—leaves the student under a great misapprehension. He fails to grasp that colonization was a specifically Christian enterprise and that one of the stated purposes of colonization in every charter granted by the Crown was the propagation of the Gospel.[6]

The Puritans are often referred to—usually in a pejorative manner—but they are almost never identified. Who they were, what they believed, and where they have gone are questions which are not seriously addressed. Bryan also mentions the frequent and inexcusable neglect of the importance of the First Great Awakening and the common omission of any reference to such persons as Increase or Cotton Mather, John Eliot, or Jonathan Edwards. Of course, he does not discuss these books' treatment of religion after 1700, since such treatment hardly exists in any scholarly form.

With the exception of the presentation of religion, especially in the Colonial Period, in the 1979 Addison-Wesley text (by Madgic, Seaburg, Stopsky, and Winks)—a book not in Bryan's sample—and a few other isolated cases, there is little in our own findings that can brighten Bryan's dismal conclusions.

FIVE

The Stories in Our Children's Readers

THIS CHAPTER INVESTIGATES how religion and other values are represented in the books used to teach reading, known as basal readers. These books primarily use stories—often fiction, but nature, science, and biographical pieces as well—to develop students' reading ability. The content of these stories and articles is an important source of values and information for students, and it is the concern of this study. Obviously readers, unlike social studies and history texts, have no direct obligation to report historical fact. However, educators have long realized the importance of stories for the teaching of values and attitudes. Thus, these stories should reinforce the values, goals, and attitudes widely shared by American parents. The stories should also refrain from attacking beliefs or values held as important by any large segment of the American public. Certainly if the readers deal with politically and socially controversial issues, all major sides of the issue should be given representation.

Sample. For the following reasons, only the readers for grades 3 and 6 were selected for study. The material in many grade 1 and 2 readers is in the form of short paragraphs, single sentences, and lists of words (vocabulary) associated with pictures. The students are still learning to read in these grades. The grade 3 readers are, however, primarily composed of stories and short articles, making them the first real readers. The readers for grades 7 and 8 were excluded since they are not that widely used. Various collections of stories are often substituted at these higher grades, making grade 7 and 8 basal readers relatively unrepresentative of what is read in these grades. Therefore, the highest grade level reader selected for the sample was the grade 6 basal reader. Grades 4 and 5 were not sampled because they are very similar to grades 3 and 6. Indeed, professionals familiar with basal readers thought that sampling one grade level, e.g., 5 or 6, would provide an adequate and representative sample of the content of the stories. As a result, the two grades, 3 and 6, are more than adequate.

The particular books used in the sample are shown in Table 7. The sample in Table 7 is a representative one. The eleven publishers selected are all either on the official adoption list of California or of Texas. The sample is also representative of those texts adopted by other states. There are ten other states with official adoptions of basal readers whose lists were made available by EPIE in time for this study. The Table 7 texts represent a substantial proportion of the officially adopted readers from these other states.

Specifically, the present sample accounts for the following percent of the adopted readers for the states as listed: Alabama, 73%; Arkansas, 78%; Florida, 80%; Georgia, 77%; Idaho, 85%; Mississippi, 100%; Nevada, 78%; North Carolina, 83%; Virginia, 62%; and West Virginia, 69%. On average, the sample accounts for 78.4% of all adopted textbooks for these ten states— and, of course, 100% of California and Texas. If one assumes the adoption states are similar to the thirty-eight nonadoption states, then the sample texts of this study could account for approximately 80% of the basal readers used in the country for grades 3 and 6. This estimate is probably too high since some states use the same books but with different copyright dates. Some states apparently have somewhat larger adoption lists than EPIE was able to provide. There is another minor qualification to be made as to the sample. Most of the publishers shown in Table 7 publish two or sometimes three basal readers for each grade, representing two or three different levels of difficulty. In such cases, the book for the sample was selected at random from the two or three possible texts. In addition, several of the readers not in the sample

Table 7

Publishers, Copyright Dates, Titles, and Grade Levels of the Basal Readers
Used in Study Five

Publisher—Copyright	Titles and Grade Level
1. Allyn & Bacon (1978)	*Hand Stands* (3) *Standing Strong* (6)
2. Economy (1978) (Keytexts)	*Turnstyles* (3) *Forerunners* (6)
3. Ginn (1984)	*Ten Times Round* (3) *Golden Voyages* (6)
4. Harcourt Brace Jovanovich (1983)	*Ring Around the World* (3) *Flights of Color* (6)
5. Heath (1983)	*Catching Glimpses* (3) *Making Choices* (6)
6. Holt, Rinehart & Winston (1983)	*Never Give Up* (3) *Riders on the Earth* (6)
7. Houghton Mifflin (1983)	*Spinners* (3) *Beacons* (6)
8. Laidlaw Brothers (1984)	*Whispering Ghosts* (3) *Voyages* (6)
9. Lippincott (1981)	*Zooming Ahead* (3) *Flying High* (6)
10. Macmillan (1983)	*Full Circle* (3) *Catch the Wind* (6)
11. Scott, Foresman (1983)	*Golden Secrets* (3) *Star Fight* (6)

were reviewed—and they were remarkably similar to those included. At any rate, the present sample is widely representative of the country and of most, if not all, states.

Scoring. Only stories or articles were scored. Thus, poems, plays, games, exercises, reviews, and similar material were not evaluated. Such items, however, were always a relatively small part of the total content of each book, since stories and articles usually took up anywhere from 75% to 90% of the pages. A story or article could be ordinary fiction or historical fiction; factual, such as a nature article; or a mixture of fact and fiction, as in most of the biographies in these readers. To score, the author or an assistant read each story or article in each book and wrote a brief summary. All references to religion were specifically noted. Later the author read all the stories and articles scored by the assistant to gain firsthand familiarity with the complete sample. The summaries of the 670 items (stories and articles) scored in these twenty-two books can be found in Appendix D of the original report.

The independent analyst read all the stories in four of the readers to check on the accuracy of the authors' summaries. The four were selected randomly: two from grade 3 (Allyn & Bacon and Harcourt Brace Jovanovich) and two from grade 6 (Houghton Mifflin and Scott, Foresman). This analyst found only one story out of 140 that had a reference to religion of any significance that was missed by the author. This story had one sentence that mentioned the "good Lord." Thus, although a few stray religious references still might have been missed in the 670-item sample, these possible oversights would not change any of the major conclusions. In addition, each of the conclusions and results mentioned below was evaluated for accuracy by the same independent evaluator.

General Character of the Stories

We are all familiar with the kind of music known as muzak. This is the uniform, unobtrusive, somewhat mushy music one hears played in the background at supermarkets, department stores, and when our telephone call has been put on hold. The great majority of these stories and articles are also uniform, unobtrusive, sentimental, and filled with easy vocabulary and simplified expression. That is, the majority of these pieces are to literature what muzak is to music, or what fast food is to real food. In addition, each publisher is very like the others—for example, there is little to distinguish one grade 3 book from another.

The stories themselves are of various types. Fictional stories entirely about animals or about humans preoccupied with animals account for roughly 13% of the sample; another 7% are articles about animals but are of an informative, natural history type, including stories about scientists involved with animals. Thus, roughly 20% of the 670 items are animal stories of some kind. Biographical pieces—often a kind of historical fiction—plus fictional stories about personal achievement accounted for another 20% of the sample. About 18% of the stories deal with interpersonal relationships, emotions, facing tensions, and school-based social adjustment difficulties. About 16% of the stories are fairy tales, myths, fables, or science fiction; 10% are adventure stories, either true, e.g., *Kon-Tiki,* or fictional. (This excludes adventures that are biographical or focused on animals since these were counted in those categories.) The remaining 16% consist primarily of articles of an informative kind on various topics and some miscellaneous categories.

Treatment of Religion

To all intents and purposes, religion is excluded from these basal readers. There is not one story or article in all these books, in approximately nine to ten thousand pages, in which the central motivation or major content derives from Christianity or Judaism. Religious motivation is a significant, although quite secondary, concern in only five or six stories or articles—less than 1% of the stories. In a few instances, religion is part of a story in a minor or peripheral way but without any narrative importance.

No informative article deals with religion as a primary subject worthy of treatment. There are scores of articles about animals, archaeology, fossils, or about magic—but none on religion, much less any about Christianity. In contrast to the serious neglect of Christianity and also Judaism, there is a minor spiritual or occult emphasis in a number of stories about American Indians. One fifty-five page story featured a typical white American girl on a ranch in California who seeks to find her "Indian Heart" (Laidlaw: 6). The girl makes several animal fetishes and understands a fetish as capturing the spirit of the animal, in this case, the coyote. She seeks ways to commune with animal spirits as part of her search for her "Indian Heart." Another story, "Medicine Bag," (Laidlaw:6; Lippincott:6) features an Indian medicine bag passed on from father to son; the bag is part of an Indian youth's "Vision Quest" in which he seeks the meaning of his name. An article about Comanche medicine art gives not only interpretation of the artist's paintings but also information about Indian spirituality (Economy, grade 6). In this article misleading comparisons are made with the Bible. For example, "A prophet [in the Bible] was said to have come from another world, or Heaven, to give People on Earth vision, or a reason for being... people you call saints or disciples wrote down what they 'saw' through your prophets" (p. 87).

This quote implies that prophets come from another world—hardly an accurate representation of the Judeo-Christian concept of the prophet. Perhaps the author is referring to Jesus as a prophet, but if so this raises even more disturbing issues.

But for a more detailed picture of how religion is treated, consider the following descriptions of those few stories that do mention Christianity or Judaism. First, a biography of the Mayo brothers and their establishment of the Mayo Clinic mentions that an order of Catholic nuns was instrumental in setting up the Mayos' first hospital, called St. Mary's (Allyn & Bacon:3). Second, a story featuring Joliet and Marquette mentions that the latter was a Catholic priest (Heath:3), and a story on the animals of China mentions a French priest-naturalist, Fr. David (Houghton Mifflin:6). Third, one story mentions an Hispanic artist who, among other things, drew a nativity scene (Economy:6); an article on masks mentions masks in South American religious festivals at Mardi Gras and Lent (Allyn & Bacon:6). Keep in mind that in these stories the actual numbers of lines containing such a religious reference is small and that these references are descriptive—without reference to clear religious motivation. Thus these references are to secondary aspects of religion. The exception to this is a story about the famous battle at the Alamo, which is described as a mission church in Texas, and a young boy's mention of his family's church and Our Lady of Guadalupe. The boy's mother prayed for the safety of her Hispanic husband, the boy's father, during the battle (Houghton Mifflin:6). The religious meaning of these actions, however, is somewhat ambiguous since the mother's prayers were ineffectual and her husband is killed along with the rest of the defenders.

A story by the Jewish writer Isaac Bashevis Singer set in nineteenth century eastern Europe in a small village has something of a religious theme (Macmillan:6). It takes place during Hanukkah and involves a Jewish boy and the family goat who get lost for three days in a blizzard. The boy is saved by finding a haystack in which to sit out the storm and by the goat who keeps him warm and supplies milk. After the storm he returns home. The celebration of Hanukkah provides an important background for the story, but the religious and political meaning of Hanukkah is not given, and for most readers it could be just an unexplained ethnic holiday.

There is also a brief selection from a story about two Jewish girls hidden in the home of a Dutch farmer during World War II (Macmillan:6). That the girls are Jewish is mentioned once; there is no other reference to religion.

There is another Jewish story that centers on the mother making gefilte fish (from a live carp kept in the bathtub) for Passover (Allyn & Bacon:3). God is mentioned once, but no reference is made to the religious meaning of Passover, and the focus of the article is on the poor fish! Passover, like Hanukkah in the previous story, could be a strictly secular ethnic holiday as far as the text is concerned.

Religion receives a neutral or positive brief mention in a few stories on black history or black life. One story refers to information in the family Bible of Benjamin Banneker (Lippincott:6); another (Houghton Mifflin:6) refers to the "good Lord" once; and a story about a black teenager who buys and repairs an inner city house mentions that his father was a minister (Economy:6). A third story is a history of the origin and development of jazz (by far one of the better pieces in all the twenty-two books). This history correctly and positively identifies the importance of the black church for the development of black music (Lippincott:6). A story about anthropologists in Africa mentions that missionaries brought Christianity to some members of the tribe (Holt, Rinehart & Winston:6). A story on Harriet Tubman helping slaves escape via the underground railway mentions her prayer to the Lord and that two ministers, one a Quaker, are important in the escape (Houghton Mifflin:6). Finally, there is an account of the life of Martin Luther King, Jr. that mentions he was a minister, discusses his going to seminary, and quotes his "thank God, I'm free at last" speech (Houghton Mifflin:6).

One piece has a preface explaining that the story is about a Mennonite family in America that fled Russia to avoid religious persecution (Houghton Mifflin:6)—but who the Mennonites are is not explained. A story about pioneer life on the prairie describes Christmas as a warm time for special foods (Houghton Mifflin:6). This is really not a religious reference since the text calls Christmas a time for "thought and thanksgiving," and no religious meaning is given. One tale of King Arthur refers briefly to the Bible, a cathedral, and an archbishop (Holt, Rinehart & Winston:6).

In the preceding examples, one sees the same pattern found in the social studies textbooks: (1) no major Christian or Jewish religious motivation is ever shown, and there is virtually no serious representation of religion; (2) there is the complete omission of any typical active Protestantism, but a small number of "minority" religions, e.g., Catholic, Jewish, Black, Mennonite, do get a few positive representations; and (3) the rare references to religion are mostly descriptive and neutral, and they are secondary religious references (as in Table 3). For example, even in the relatively religious biographical piece on Martin Luther King, Jr., there is no reference to how Christian ideas or the life of Jesus affected him. (The name Jesus doesn't occur once in these 670 stories.)

There are two stories that each contain one sentence mentioning a major character praying at a time of extreme danger: one, when two boys think they are lost on an iceflow; the other, when a boat carrying immigrants from Ireland has trouble in a storm (Houghton Mifflin:6, p. 427; Laidlaw:6). Again, no reference is made as to whom the characters are praying, however. And finally there is another story in which a man, delighted in being rescued after days of living alone on a large iceberg, shouts in German, "Gott im Himmel" (Houghton Mifflin:6). But the translation of the words is not given.

In addition, there are a few references to God or Christianity that are critical or implicitly negative. There is a story of Maria Mitchell, a woman astronomer in nineteenth century America, with a strong feminist message. When the character visits the Vatican Observatory, the story refers somewhat critically to Christianity in the context of the trial of Galileo. This story also refers to "The Book of Nature and the Book of God," implying that nature is not also the book of God (Lippincott:6).

In a story about Columbus's first voyage, he finally discovers, after much struggle and anxiety, the New World and names the island San Salvador. This expression is the only Spanish in the story, yet it is not translated or explained. A story on the life of the Spanish explorer Estevan mentions that every few days he sent a message back to the rest of his Spanish party by way of the local Indians. He sent a small cross (two sticks tied together) if he had found things of minor interest and a large cross if a major discovery had occurred. The cross is, in this case, a sign with no religious meaning. (Both of the above stories are in Harcourt Brace Jovanovich:3.) There is also a science fiction story (Holt, Rinehart & Winston:6), set in the southern mountains of the United States, that refers to church-goers in a critical context.

Religions other than Christianity or Judaism receive relatively frequent mention. For example, Greek or Roman religion is an important part of six stories; ancient Egyptian, Polynesian, and other pagan religions are featured in six additional stories; two stories, not especially religious, are attributed to Buddha. American Indian religion is emphasized quite positively in five stories and one article. But no Bible stories occur in these books, not even that of David and Goliath.

Curiously, there is something of an emphasis on magic in these books. For example, thirteen stories (2% of the total) feature magic, e.g., how to do it (Allyn & Bacon:6; Economy:3; Ginn:6; Lippincott:3,3; Lippincott:6; Scott, Foresman:3,3); magicians, e.g., Harry Houdini (Economy:3; Ginn:6; Harcourt Brace Jovanovich:6); sorcery, e.g., the "Sorcerer's Apprentice" (Allyn & Bacon:3; Lippincott:6). In addition, many other stories have magic as central to the plot and story resolution. In short, stories referring to the occult, to magic, to Indian and other pagan religions are featured about five times more often than stories which mention anything of a Judeo-Christian nature.

Finally, let us note the books which are especially weak or strong in their treatment of traditional religion. The following texts either had no reference at all or only minor (neutral or negative) references to God, Christianity, or Judaism: Allyn & Bacon:6; Economy:3 and 6; Ginn:3 and 6; Harcourt Brace Jovanovich:3 and 6; Heath:3 and 6; Holt, Rinehart & Winston:3; Houghton Mifflin:3; Laidlaw:3; Lippincott:3; Macmillan:3; Scott, Foresman:3 and 6. *That is, sixteen of twenty-two books, or 72%, completely fail even a minimum test with respect to reference to God, Christianity, or Judaism.* Of the remaining books, five contain a few very modest references. *Beacons* (Houghton Mifflin:6) had by far the largest number of stories presenting God and Christianity. It has nothing on Judaism or representative Protestantism, but it does introduce religion into eight of the book's forty pieces, and thus it is clearly the best of those analyzed.

Other biases in these 670 stories and articles relevant to the present study are also of note.

1. *Lack of patriotism.* There are only five stories in all these books with any patriotic theme. Three of the five instances describe the story of the ride of Sybil Ludington in 1777. Dressed as a man, she warned local pro-Independence farmers about a British threat (Allyn & Bacon:6; Houghton Mifflin:6; Macmillan:6). This story is in many respects a feminist piece and it has little of a specifically patriotic character. There is another Revolutionary War story about Mary, a black girl who wants to join the army and who helps bring food to George Washington's troops during the harsh winter at Valley Forge (Holt, Rinehart & Winston:3); and a story about an American boy during the Revolutionary War who captures a British soldier who was stealing vegetables from his garden (Scott, Foresman:6). To summarize: of the twenty-two textbooks, seventeen (over 75%)

do not have one patriotic story. Furthermore, none of the patriotic stories has anything to do with American history since 1780—nothing for the last two hundred years. Four of the five stories feature girls and are certainly at least as feminist in orientation as they are patriotic. Only one book out of twenty-two—one story out of 670—has a story with a patriotic theme that features a boy. These books do not have one story featuring Nathan Hale, Patrick Henry, Daniel Boone, or Paul Revere's ride.

2. *Lack of support for business.* Only two stories (or articles) have a business theme of any kind. There is an article about a black youth who buys a house in a run-down part of town, fixes it up, and becomes the youngest landlord in Michigan (Economy:6). Here, the emphasis is on good citizenship—and on succeeding as a young black teenager; the emphasis on business success is secondary.

There are no stories about Henry Ford, Andrew Carnegie, or any more recent examples of this type, such as Lee Iacocca. Neither is there a single story in which an immigrant to this country finds—along with religious freedom—happiness and success in business or in a profession. However, one long story (Holt, Rinehart & Winston:6, p. 143) refers disparagingly to money, profit, and free enterprise.

The only real business success story is one that features Maggie Mitchell Walker, a black woman from Richmond, Virginia, born in 1867. This story, which appears in three different readers (Heath:6; Holt, Rinehart & Winston:6; Scott, Foresman:6), does make the point that she became a successful banker, but the major emphasis is feminist. Her accomplishment is in overcoming the prejudice of black men against black women. (No white prejudice against blacks is noted since all the characters in the story are black.) Even if these two stories are counted as pro-business or pro-free enterprise, they comprise less than 1% of the stories and articles. Three times more stories feature magic than feature hard work and success in business.

It is also worth pointing out that there are no stories about labor or labor unions.

In conclusion, then, these stories grossly underrepresent this country's workers and, in particular, our entrepreneurial business spirit. Indeed, about those Americans who have built and are still building our major industries and businesses there is not a single word.

3. *Lack of altruism.* There are no stories that feature helping others or being concerned for others as intrinsically meaningful and valuable. The few stories that do involve concern for others— i.e., for family or country—really turn the spotlight on the individual and his or her accomplishment. For example, no one dies for his or her family or country, much less for faith. No character in any story articulates a strong belief in the intrinsic value of altruism. Over and over the emphasis is on individual success. The motivation expressed by a Charles Colson in his prison ministry, or by members of the Salvation Army, or by Fr. Bruce Ritter in his ministry to runaways, or by Dorothy Day or Mother Teresa of Calcutta is completely absent in all 670 stories. Surprisingly, not even the many secular saints, such as Jane Addams, who have expressed a concern for the poor are represented. In short, these are stories for the "me generation"— stories that express and perpetuate what Christopher Lasch so aptly describes as the "culture of narcissism"—a culture heavily

Figure 5:1

"WE'RE NOT INSTILLING GOOD CHARACTER TRAITS IN KIDS?! BUT WE GOT RID OF EVERYTHING THAT WOULD HURT THEIR LITTLE MINDS... PRAYER, CREATION SCIENCE AND BIBLE STUDIES!"

supported by contemporary social science and educational theory.[1]

4. *A feminist emphasis.* By far the most noticeable ideological position in the readers is a feminist one. This shows in a number of ways. To begin with, certain themes just do not occur in these stories and articles. Hardly a story celebrates motherhood or marriage as a positive goal or as a rich and meaningful way of living. The few with a modest promotherhood emphasis are set in the past or involve ethnic mothers. No story clearly supports motherhood for today's woman. No story shows any woman or girl with a positive relationship to a baby or young child; no story deals with a girl's positive relationship with a doll; no picture shows a girl with a baby or a doll. This absence of any positive portrayal of traditional womanhood is clear evidence of bias.

Even romance receives short shrift. Only five stories focused on any form of romantic love—and one involved two dogs (Macmillan:3)! Another is an O. Henry story about a young man and woman who have fallen out over a misunderstanding (Lippincott:6), and a third features a young black girl who daydreams that a popular singer will fall in love with her (Economy:6). A fourth story has a loving prince win the hand of a princess even though she has apparently changed into a cat (Houghton Mifflin:6). A fifth story (also Houghton Mifflin:6) involves a captured Confederate officer. His new wife (dressed as a man) tries to rescue him from prison and almost succeeds. But in the end the officer is killed, and she is caught and hanged. Her ghost is said to still haunt the area. The emphasis is more on her daring attempted rescue of her husband (feminist: the wife as hero) than on romance. In retrospect, only the O. Henry story is really a romance. Though great literature, from *Tristan and Isolde* to Shakespeare to Jane Austen to Louisa May Alcott, is filled with romance and the desire to marry, one finds very little of that in these texts.

There are, however, role reversal "romances." For example, there is a story of a princess who sets out to slay the dragon in her kingdom: she invents the first gun and with it shoots and kills the dragon. The slain dragon turns into a prince who asks the princess to marry him. She rather casually agrees but only if her new kingdom has lots of dragons in it for her to slay and lots of drawbridges for her to fix. She wants to keep busy at such things ("Young Ladies Don't Slay Dragons," Holt, Rinehart & Winston:6). There is not one story of a prince rescuing a princess or slaying a dragon. In these readers, no man saves or even attempts to save a woman.

Stories set in the past and featuring sex role reversal are very common, as are parodies of traditional stories about kings and queens or about young men rescuing maidens. Examples are: "The Queen Who Changed Places with the King" (Scott, Foresman:3); "The Practical Princess" (Holt, Rinehart & Winston:3); "The Queen Who Couldn't Bake Gingerbread" (Ginn:3); "Castle under the Sea" (Ginn:6); "The Last of the Dragons" (Lippincott:6); "The Princess and the Admiral" (Allyn & Bacon:6); "Trouble in Camelot" (Holt, Rinehart & Winston:6). The last three stories are especially hostile toward men and male roles.

The frequent stories of female successes in these books are all in traditional male activities and are told in very masculine vocabulary. For example, there are many stories about women fliers, e.g., Amelia Earhart, Harriet Quimby (Ginn:6; Harcourt Brace Jovanovich:3; Laidlaw:6; Lippincott:6; Macmillan:6). There is only one story on the Wright Brothers—and it is one page long (Macmillan:6); nothing on Charles Lindberg or any other male aviation pioneers. The stories about women pilots use such words as *courage,* and *daring,* while stories about men almost never use this vocabulary.

There are also explicitly feminist stories, such as those about leaders in the women's movement, e.g., Elizabeth Blackwell, the first female M.D. (Allyn & Bacon:6), and Elizabeth Cady Stanton (Houghton Mifflin:6). These stories about real feminists are much more factual than the feminist fiction pieces and address an important historical movement. Because they are honest and straightforward in their purpose, they contrast sharply with the manipulative and wish fulfillment quality of the many other feminist stories and articles.

Other examples of strongly feminist stories are the following: a story about a new kid on the block who wins at "King of the Hill" and other boyish activities but who turns out to be a girl (Allyn & Bacon:3); a dog sled race between a girl and a boy where the girl turns back to rescue the boy when he gets in trouble and still manages to beat him to the finish line (Harcourt Brace Jovanovich:3); a story of the star baseball player—a girl—wno is in a hitting slump because her favorite Rusty McGraw bat is missing. Her friend, a girl detective, solves the problem by finding that a boy has stolen it so he could make the first team instead of the girl. At the end she gets her bat back and hits two home runs (Heath:3). Stories showing competition, especially physical competition between girls and boys, almost always have the girl winning. In short, stories about "Wonder Woman and the Wlmp" are common throughout these books while traditional sex roles are almost entirely excluded. Another example is the story in two readers of the girl trail boss who drives longhorn cattle back from Texas to Illinois (Ginn:6 and Laidlaw:6).

There are other types of feminist bias in these books, such as stories that rewrite or misrepresent history by referring to women judges, merchants, and soldiers at times and places where, in fact, there weren't any. In one astonishing instance, an Encyclopedia Brown mystery is rewritten. (Encyclopedia Brown is a boy detective in a series of stories that are popular with children.) The rewritten story changes Encyclopedia to a girl (Laidlaw:3). Some kind of feminist emphasis characterizes approximately 10% of the stories and articles in the sample, that is, sixty-five items, and the bias is especially heavy-handed in at least many of them. As already noted there are no equivalent stories representing traditional concepts of womanhood. Likewise, countless parents wanting clear male role models for their sons will not find them in these books.

Conclusions

When one looks at the total sample of 670 pieces in these basal readers, the following findings stand out. Serious Judeo-Christian religious motivation is featured nowhere. References to Christianity or Judaism are rare and generally superficial. Protestantism is almost entirely excluded, at least for whites. In contrast, primitive and pagan religions, as well as magic, get considerable emphasis. Patriotism is close to nonexistent in the sample. Likewise, any appreciation of business success is grossly unrepresented. Traditional roles for both men and women receive virtually no support, but feminist portrayals regularly show women engaged in activities indistinguishable from those of men. Finally, clear attacks on traditional sex roles, especially traditional concepts of manhood, are common.

SIX

What Should Be Done?

T HESE STUDIES make it abundantly clear that public school textbooks commonly exclude the history, heritage, beliefs, and values of millions of Americans. Those who believe in the traditional family are not represented. Those who believe in free enterprise are not represented. Those whose politics are conservative are almost unrepresented. Above all, those who are committed to their religious tradition—at the very least as an important part of the historical record—are not represented.

Even those who uphold the classic or republican virtues of discipline, public duty, hard work, patriotism, and concern for others are scarcely represented. Indeed, the world of these virtues long advocated by believers, as well as by deists and skeptics such as Thomas Paine, Benjamin Franklin, and Thomas Jefferson, is not found here. Even what one might call the "noble pagan" has ample reason to reject these inadequate and sentimentalized books which seem to be about an equal mixture of pap and propaganda.

Over and over, we have seen that liberal and secular bias is primarily accomplished by exclusion, by leaving out the opposing position. Such a bias is much harder to observe than a positive vilification or direct criticism, but it is the essence of censorship. It is effective not only because it is hard to observe—it isn't *there*—and therefore hard to counteract, but also because it makes only the liberal, secular positions familiar and plausible. As a result, the millions of Americans who hold conservative, traditional, and religious positions are made to appear irrelevant, strange, on the fringe, old-fashioned, reactionary. For these countless Americans it is now surely clear that the textbooks used in the public schools threaten the continued existence of their positions.

A natural question to raise is: how could this textbook bias have happened? What brought it about? Some have suggested that religion is downplayed because of concern over maintaining the separation of church and state. This concern seems either unlikely or a rationalization of an underlying distaste for religion. After all, to identify the historical or contemporary importance of religion is to respect the facts; it is not to advocate religion. To teach *about* religion is not to teach religion.

Furthermore, the rejection of religion in these books is part of a very general rejection of the entire conservative spectrum of American life. Recall that these books omit marriage and the traditional family, along with traditional sex roles, patriotism, and free enterprise. In short, the bias in these books is not accidental; much of it is certainly not the result of some misunderstanding about separating church and state.

Another possible answer is that the publishers of these books have attempted to avoid controversial subjects. According to this theory, the books have been written in a style which will avoid offending anyone. In fact, some publishers do give guidelines to authors on what kinds of people and issues to avoid. But the evidence of this study makes clear that a desire to avoid offense and controversy *cannot* explain much of the bias observed here. First, consider the role models presented in Table 5. Apparently all male Republicans are controversial while Eleanor Roosevelt and Margaret Mead are not. In short, Table 5 is filled with people who do give offense to many. Second, consider the profeminist position found in several social studies texts and throughout the basal readers for grades 3 and 6. That feminism is controversial cannot be seriously denied, even by feminists. And consider that positive representations of traditional feminine role models are obviously absent from these books. The regular procoverage of environmental issues also makes clear that the only people and topics which are avoided in these books are those on the political right, those that are "controversial" to a liberal frame of mind.

One explanation of the antireligious bias in these books is that religion is so especially controversial that publishers want to avoid the subject. Curiously, the religions that do get some mention, e.g., Catholicism, Judaism, and Islam, are hardly uncontroversial. (In any case, why religion is supposedly more controversial than race, ethnic identity, feminism, or politics remains to be explained.)

The real issue is how a book handles religion. For example, magazines like the *Reader's Digest* and others often have articles about the positive accomplishments of people of different religious denominations. Such articles celebrating the different religions and their contributions to this country are uncontroversial, well received, and appear to help sales. Yet, such a positive treatment of America's religious life is without any example in the ninety books evaluated in this entire study.

Religious concepts and vocabulary are certainly censored in these textbooks. A most revealing example of this censorship was recently published in the article "Censoring the Sources" by Barbara Cohen.[1] The issue centered on a children's story of hers called "Molly's Pilgrim." The story has an important Jewish religious theme; it focuses on the Jewish harvest holiday of Sukkos, a holiday that influenced the Pilgrims in initiating Thanksgiving. A major textbook publisher (Harcourt Brace Jovanovich) wanted to reprint part of the story for their third grade reader. But like most such stories, the publishers wanted to shorten it greatly and to rewrite parts to make it more acceptable. They phoned Ms. Cohen and asked her for permission to reprint their modified version. But her story wasn't just modified, it was maimed. "All mention of Jews, Sukkos, God, and the Bible"[2] had been removed. So Barbara Cohen refused to give them permission. They called back dismayed and tried to convince her to let them go ahead with the heavily censored version. They argued, "Try to understand. We have a lot of problems. If we mention God, some atheist will object. If we mention the Bible, someone will want to know why we don't give equal time to the Koran. Every time that happens, we lose sales."[3] "But the Pilgrims did read the Bible," Barbara Cohen answered.[4] Yes, you know that and we know that, but we can't have anything in it that people object to, was the reply!

After more debate and give and take, a compromise was

reached. The publisher allowed a reference to worship and the Jewish harvest holiday of Sukkos to stay in. But God and the Bible were "eternally unacceptable"[5] and they had to go. The publisher claimed, "We'll get into terrible trouble if we mentioned the Bible."[6]

This true but incredible story ends with Barbara Cohen stating: "Censorship in this country is widespread, subtle, and surprising. It is not inflicted on us by the government. It doesn't need to be. We inflict it on ourselves."[7] At the very least, the publishers should hear from the millions of Christians and Jews that if God and the Bible are left out, the publishers will also lose sales. And, God willing, lots more sales will be lost than when publishers leave God and the Bible in. The schools and the publishers must learn that what is left out of a textbook can be just as offensive as what is let in.

Of course, the central issue hinges on the *facts* of America's past and present. And the facts are clear: religion, especially Christianity, has played and continues to play a central role in American life. To neglect to report this is simply to fail to carry out the major duty of any textbook writer—the duty to tell the truth.

To explain the liberal and secular prejudice of the texts, some have proposed that a deliberate, large-scale conspiracy is involved. I doubt very much, however, that this is the case. The number of people writing, editing, publishing, selecting, and using these books is far too large and varied for this explanation to be plausible. Instead, the bias is, I believe, the consequence of the widespread, dominant, secular worldview found throughout the upper levels of the field of education,[8] especially among those who control the schools of education, the publishers, the federal and state education bureaucracies, and the National Education Association. But, whatever the source of the bias, it certainly exists. Thus, the question is "What should be done?" Let us consider the major possibilities.

One possibility that I will call *Scenario One* is as follows. In this possible future the public school leadership acknowledges that the majority of America's parents are religious in their sympathies and generally conservative in their moral and social life. Recognizing this, educators move clearly and positively back into the mainstream of American life. Religion is given a positive and realistic portrayal in textbooks and other curriculum. The traditional family and moral values are recognized and integrated into the school programs. Finally, the new emphasis on character education continues to grow and become widely influential.

The result of making these changes is a revival of confidence in the public schools and increased community support. As a result, many religious Americans return their children to the public schools. Meanwhile more secular Yuppy parents note the increased morale of teachers and students and they also return to active public school support. After all, the private schools favored by many of the young upwardly mobile professionals are quite expensive. Revitalized public schools would be welcomed by many of them. In short, in this scenario the public schools are positively transformed and gain a new long lease on life.

Unfortunately, another possibility—one I call *Scenario Two*—appears much more likely. The logic of this alternative is more complex; it goes roughly as follows.

Reform the Textbooks?

Scenario Two begins with a focus on textbook reform. After all, it is the books that are bad, so why not try to improve them? But what is likely to make the publishers change? Certainly not criticism by itself. Publishers will change only if it costs them money to continue with their present books and policies. At present, yearly sales of textbooks to public schools total nearly a billion dollars.[9] No publisher will jeopardize present profits by changing unless forced to.

A crucial aspect of any possible textbook reform is to understand how these books are produced. The most easily grasped description of the textbook process that I have found is the cartoon (Figure 6:1) shown here. The picture is humorous because it is so accurate. Of course, the system could use more conservative pressure groups, a religion processing gizmo, and a more traditional role model mix. But let's face it, the whole process is a disaster. School textbooks are never written by something as simple as one author, not even by one committee. They are written by a whole series of committees. Forgetting the issue of biased content, the present process also removes much of the intellectual content of most school books. That is, intellectual depth and basic conceptual coherence is removed by the present set of procedures. The evidence for this has been thoroughly documented by Harriet Tyson-Bernstein, Arthur Woodward, Catherine Carter Nagel, David Elliott, and other education researchers.[10] Patching up the present process is a fool's errand. Instead, some radical changes are needed.

Figure 6:1

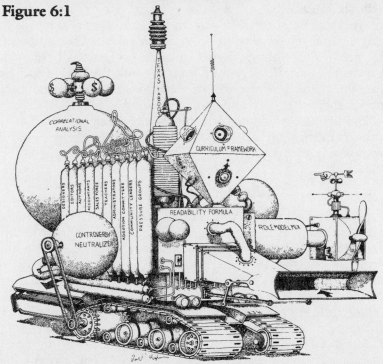

Of course, even with the present system there *could* be some modest positive change. If critics band together to create effective lobbies and if parents and some educators begin to select books from other publishers who put out more accurate and representative books, then the major publishers might begin to change a little. Lawsuits also might provide a real stimulus. The logic of such lawsuits is simple and fairly familiar. Some years ago, black Americans rightfully complained about being left out of textbooks, and the courts readily understood that such a neglect of black life and history is racist. By the same logic, leaving out the positions noted in the previous chapters is a serious form of censorship and bias. Our present textbooks, therefore, are as antireligious as our earlier books were racist. In fact, several court cases involve lawsuits based on this general logic, that is, public school agencies responsible for textbooks are being sued for having selected textbooks with antireligious bias.

If parents protest and if teachers and school administrators search for better books, then after some years and much effort there could be some changes in the overall process of textbook development, in the "Great American Textbook Machine." The new textbooks would mention a few more religious events and religiously important people. We could expect that here and there a traditional value would be advocated in a story or in a social studies section. Even a conservative political issue or politician might slip into some of the books. But in this scenario such changes would be superficial—mere tokenism. The fact remains that the people who control most of the education establishment show little evidence that they believe in traditional values and they would resist these changes. It is probable that only enough material to deflect the major criticisms would be permitted. It is simply not possible to force a system to teach facts, much less perspectives or values, opposed by most of the system's leadership. Very simply, if federal and state education bureaucrats, professors of education, and district superintendents are not sufficiently committed to maintaining the traditional family structure, traditional values, or the importance of religion, there is simply no way that they will seriously implement such ideas. Thus, textbook reform by itself—that is, serious change in the school curriculum—is impossible. It seems that the school system itself must be reformed.

Reform the Public Schools?

This suggestion makes those who know the public school system roll their eyes in disbelief—and despair. Over the years, many waves of reform have washed over the schools with very little to show for any of them.[11] The net result has been that the schools are either unchanged or worse. A number of major characteristics of today's public schools account for this and imply that Scenario Two is the more likely future response of the public school system. The following list identifies some of these characteristics in order to document the inherent unreformability of the public schools—and to point out the futility of reform as a way to remove bias from textbooks.

1. *The increase in the size and the amount of educational bureaucracy.* One of the truly major changes in the schools in recent decades has been their great centralization and the resulting increase in bureaucracy. For example, in 1931-1932, there were approximately 259,000 separate school districts in the country; by 1980, there were only about 16,000.[12] This fifteen-fold drop has occurred while the number of students has increased by the millions. The result, as countless chagrined parents have discovered, is loss of local control. The schools no longer respond to parents or taxpayers; they respond to their own bureaucrats, that is, to the federal and state systems that more or less control and support the schools. Such a huge bureaucratized system, primarily concerned with complex and changing laws and regulations, has almost no real capacity for any kind of internal, positive change.

2. *The local educator's loss of authority.* In recent years, local educators not only have lost power and authority to federal and state bureaucrats, they also have lost much of it to political and legal forces altogether outside the schools. An example taken from the work of Joseph Adelson, one of the many recent insightful and articulate critics of our schools, illustrates this.[13] The incidents in question took place several years ago in Adelson's hometown.[14]

The first instance involved older children who were bullying and extorting money from younger children on the way to and from junior high school. The complaints to the principal were ineffective, so a PTA meeting was called. It was a rancorous meeting in which the parents were given a summary of the legal restrictions standing in the way of any kind of corrective action by the school authorities. That is, the parents were told why the school principal couldn't do anything about the problem.

Adelson described the parents as "incredulous, then angry and disgusted."[15]

The second example involved the case of black English.[16] The case started when a group of radical activists, mostly white, sued the school system on behalf of a group of black families. They claimed that the poor academic progress of the blacks was due to the fact that their native language was black English while standard English was used in the schools. The solution was for teachers to be trained to use and respect black English. Adelson notes that to those on the scene the proposed position seemed frivolous. For example, there was no evidence that black children spoke black English exclusively, or that they couldn't understand standard English. After all, these black children watched television daily and talked easily with their white classmates. Those who really knew these children reported "that black English is a variant dialect that can be turned on and off depending on the circumstances, in much the same way that many middle class Southern children learn to speak both standard English and 'country.'"[17] Adelson goes on to note, however, that a federal judge decided to hear the case. To the community's astonishment, he decided that black English was a factor in these children's poor performance. The remedy ordered was to require teachers to attend lectures on black English. Subsequent tests showed that this remedial program for teachers made no difference in the children's performance.

Adelson concludes:

> What should trouble us most about this case is the ease with which a judge has intruded himself into the heart of the educator's domain, into what is to be taught, how it is to be taught, and how teachers are to be trained to teach it. What qualifies the judge to do so? What qualifies him to pronounce on the linguistics of English dialects? What qualifies him to pronounce on the causes of scholastic achievement, and the means needed to enhance it? The answer is—nothing at all. . . .[18]

These examples exemplify the loss of control and authority that school administrators have suffered. Such a system could not reform itself even if it wanted to for the simple reason that it doesn't control itself. The schools are no longer autonomous, even with respect to the basic issues of discipline or curriculum content.

3. *The antitraditional values of the education leadership.* A major reason for not expecting change is that many leaders of the public schools seem to be personally opposed to traditional values and seem much less religious than the public at large. For years the philosophy of education dominating the country's schools of education has been uniformly liberal, secular, and even antireligious. This should not be surprising; years ago, John Dewey's philosophy came to dominate American education, most especially our schools of education. From these schools, his ideas spread to principals and teachers until now Dewey's position is ubiquitous. And Dewey himself was strongly hostile to traditional religion with its belief in a transcendent reality and in revelation. For Dewey, of course, traditional religion primarily meant Christianity. Dewey was an acknowledged leader in what has since been called secular humanism, a movement officially launched with a *Humanist Manifesto* in 1933, a manifesto that was largely the consequence of Dewey's energy and prestige.[19]

Since then, countless other secularists have furthered the movement to control educational philosophy and practice. Examples of important psychologists with major impact on the schools of education are Carl Rogers and B.F. Skinner—both well known humanists hostile to traditional religion.[20] Their impact on counseling and learning theories has been nothing less than immense. The secularization of moral education is best shown by Lawrence Kohlberg[21] and the values clarification theorists Raths and Simon.[22] All of these academics are well known humanists. Whether one calls it secular humanism, enlightenment universalism, skeptical modernism, or just plain permissive liberalism, the bottom line is that a very particular and narrow sectarian philosophy has taken control of American education. This philosophy is one that occupies a small part of the American ideological and political spectrum. Besides excluding most of the usual conservative viewpoints, it rejects much of libertarianism; it also rejects some of the still more radical positions on the left.

Given the overwhelming secular philosophies characterizing American education in the last fifty years, it is to be expected that leaders in education will now differ markedly from the general American public in the area of basic moral values. This has been documented in the *Connecticut Mutual Life Report on American Values in the 80s*,[23] where, for example, it is reported that 65% of the general public describe abortion as morally wrong while only 26% of education leaders describe it as wrong; 74% of our education leaders say that abortion is "not a moral issue."[24] Likewise on many other traditional values and moral issues, the education leaders are reported to be markedly more liberal than the public. Education leaders, for example, overwhelmingly say homosexuality and lesbianism are not morally wrong.[25] This report documents the case that the leaders of education are consistently more liberal than leaders of business, voluntary associations, the military, and, not surprisingly, religious leaders. It is interesting to note that government leaders had moral positions very similar to those in education.[26]

A recent Gallup Poll shows that 95% of the American public reports a belief in God (a figure that has remained unchanged since 1944 when Gallup first asked the question.) In a typical month, over 50% of Americans go to a religious service. But one would not know this from reading our school textbooks. Any approach to education that omits reference to something that is believed in by 95% of the country is very rightly called narrow and sectarian.

There are, of course, many individual teachers who do hold traditional values, conservative economic and political views, and who are religious. But they are hard put to affect education policy because their leaders, as noted above, usually hold different views than they do. In general, the typical teacher does represent typical American values—but the curriculum is primarily controlled by those at the top, and they show little regard for the mores and values of the typical teacher or parent.

Some teachers, of course, still introduce God, prayer, and traditional concepts of right and wrong into their teaching or school activities. But teachers and schools that permit them are rare and becoming more rare all the time, for such actions are probably illegal according to recent Supreme Court decisions. At any moment, complaints or lawsuits could come these teachers' way. Such teachers and schools within public education are a dying breed operating outside professional and legal support.

4. *The National Education Association.* One national teachers' union, that is, the National Education Association (or NEA), is a fourth major barrier to any reform of the public schools. Its membership of 1.5 million makes it the largest union in the country. The NEA is not only large but it is also extremely powerful and politically active. It was founded shortly after the establishment of the public schools in the middle of the last century, and the NEA has grown with the public system. Its greatest political influence has come in the last forty years or so when schools became consolidated and were removed from community roots and local control. There can be little doubt that the NEA has a secular and liberal political philosophy and that it has increasingly come to control education.[27] Indeed, the biased content of the textbooks described in chapters one through four is congruent with the politics of the NEA, and the simplest description of these textbooks is that they are a slightly watered-down version of the NEA's own political and ideological stance.

Of course, the NEA has every right to its political ideology—although it is odd that its tax-exempt status is based on a supposedly nonpolitical character. But the special point that is relevant here is that an organization with a very particular or partisan political involvement is also controlling our schools. Consequently, it would be naive to expect what is taught in the public schools to contradict the bias of the NEA. The people who write, select, and implement the textbooks are opposed to the values, beliefs, and politics that are missing from these books.

Very simply, the enormous power of the NEA makes it inconceivable that public school reform either could occur or could remedy the textbook bias identified here. In short, the optimistic Scenario One appears most unlikely.

The Real Issue: America's Cultural War

Today's conflict in the schools is really a symptom of a much deeper polarity in the country at large. This deeper conflict is between those who are religious and support traditional values and those who are secular and advocate antitraditional or modernist values.

Again, the *Connecticut Mutual Life Report on American Values in the 80s* provides good evidence for this new conflict—really a cultural war or a *Kulturkampf,* as the Germans would put it. The Connecticut Mutual report systematically surveyed the values of different kinds of American leaders and the values of the typical American. The study concludes that the older issues prevalent in the period between 1930 and 1970 have largely receded. Instead,

> . . . we are not so much a nation of rich or poor, male or female, even liberal or conservative. Rather we are increasingly a nation with different levels of religious commitment. . . . This major finding is particularly important in light of recent widespread discussion concerning the disintegration of the family, the community, the American work ethic and faith in our political institutions and leaders.[28]

Although I think the liberal vs. conservative conflict is still a strong one, it is now obvious, some years after the publication of the *Connecticut Mutual Life Report,* that religiously based political and social action is widespread and still growing. It is a grassroots movement that is now increasingly led by a new class of political and intellectual leader.

In many respects, today's culture conflict is between those still holding on to the old, receding modern world and those committed to the new, emerging post-modern period. Although the post-modern period is still ambiguous in many respects, it is already clear that much of whatever is post-modern is basically anti-modern. Since the modern period has seen the rise of secular and liberal ideas, the new post-modern era is likely to see the rise of religious and conservative ideas.

In practical terms, this is a struggle over what conceptual categories are most relevant. This means that religious and conservative Americans claim that race, ethnic group, social class, and gender are less important than a person's religious status. Is a person a believer or not? That is the question. If so, is the person an orthodox believer? That is the next question. These are the new questions and categories in today's political and cultural strife. Indeed, to be preoccupied with race, ethnic group, and gender is unconsciously to accept the ideology of the modern, secular, and liberal mentality. In contrast, the author, who is white, male, and professional, has much in common with a black or Hispanic female worker if she is a serious religious believer. Indeed, in important respects I have much more in common with her than with my fellow white male professionals who may be atheists or skeptics. What that black woman and I have in common, of course, is our faith and with it the same general worldview. The awareness of such common bonds has brought with it the development of historically unprecedented political coalitions. Today, this means that conservative Protestants, conservative Catholics, and Orthodox Jews are now typically voting together and even working together in the political world. They have in common the same God, the same commitment to family, and the same general moral values. Today, America is dividing into a new two-class society—one committed to religion and conservative, traditional values and the other committed to secular and liberal, modernist values.

In the world of education, this division into two classes is expressed in the conflicts regarding sex education programs and the providing of birth control to teenagers, discipline and drug abuse in the schools, values clarification programs, prayer in the classroom, and, of course, the content of textbooks and other material. The conflicts are taking on an increasingly political character. Therefore it is likely that an answer, the resolution of Scenario Two, also lies within the political realm.

The General Solution: Changing the Public School Monopoly

The foregoing arguments make it clear that the bias in the public schools is deeply entrenched. It cannot be corrected by any reform of the present system. In fact, even if the current mentality, which is liberal and secular, were not present, some kind of serious bias in any large organization or bureaucracy is virtually inevitable. After all, every organization must have a particular philosophy, a set of values, a common vision, in order to function. Without an agreed-upon philosophy, an organization cannot set its goals, develop morale, and move effectively to implement its policies. This means, of course, that any school system must have a reasonably homogeneous philosophy of education in order to guide its action. Thus, whatever the particular philosophy of education used to guide the public schools, this philosophy must, of necessity, coerce the children of parents who believe differently. In short, it is intrinsic to *any* monopolistic school system that it will be oppressive and coercive—especially in a country as varied as the United States. America is truly pluralistic, and we must finally recognize that today's pluralism in American life requires pluralism in American schools.

Let us recall what the central issue is: tens of millions of Americans are paying school taxes—each taxpayer is providing hundreds or even thousands of dollars a year—to support a system that fails to represent their beliefs, values, history, and heritage. Indeed, the present public schools are actively supporting antireligious positions and pushing liberal permissive values and politics. This is a serious injustice. Quite simply, it is a classic case of "taxation without representation." We are being taxed to support schools that are systematically liquidating our most cherished beliefs.

Thomas Jefferson—hardly a reliable friend of religion—stated the principle clearly when he wrote:

> To compel a man to furnish funds for the propagation of ideas he disbelieves and abhors is sinful and tyrannical.[29]

Stephen Arons, a constitutional scholar, has powerfully summarized the seriousness of this injustice in his book *Compelling Belief: The Culture of American Schooling.*[30] In this book, Arons shows that the government's control of the content of education in a school system with a captive audience of students is a serious violation of an individual's right to freely form his or her own political, social, and moral beliefs. Arons shows very clearly that public schools violate the First Amendment.

Arons is especially sympathetic to the many families who have opposed various public school policies because the schools attack their religious or political beliefs. Usually these families lose in their struggle with the schools, but Arons correctly sees the justice of their cause.

> The struggles of these families are replete with evidence of how overt and hidden curriculums affect the transmission of culture and the formation of worldview in schools. The role models teachers provide, the structure of classrooms, and of teacher-student relationships, the way in which the school is governed, the textbooks that are approved, the concepts that are tested for, the attitudes and behavior that are rewarded or punished—all convey messages about approved and rewarded values and beliefs. Parents who oppose school authorities on issues of home education, private-school standards, or the content of curriculum and library know that schooling is not value free. Scholars who have studied the process of pedagogy and the function of education know that schooling cannot be made value free. And teachers who have labored to make connections between teaching and learning know that to try to make schooling value free is to destroy the purpose of education.[31]

Arons also notes that it is the poor who suffer most from the present educational system. They get both biased and poorly taught classes. The rich can pay public school taxes and still manage to pay private school tuition. Others can move to suburbs with public schools that at least teach some skills effectively. But this, of course, means being able to buy a house and pay expensive property taxes to finance the local schools. As usual, the poor family has no such options. The local public school, especially in the inner cities, is often both an educational and a moral disaster, but poor parents have no choice but to send their children there, often at the price of an inadequate education for their children. Therefore it is not surprising that the poor are very favorably disposed toward a voucher system or other kind of process that would give them greater freedom to choose a nonpublic school.[32] Arons describes the situation as follows:

> We have created a system of school finance that provides free choice for the rich and compulsory socialization for everyone else. The present method of financing American education discriminates against the poor and the working class and even a large part of the middle class by conditioning the exercise of First Amendment rights of school choice upon an ability to pay while simultaneously eroding the ability to pay through the regressive collection of taxes used exclusively for government schools. The arrangement seems no more defensible than denying the right to vote to those who cannot afford a poll tax.[33]

The position that the public schools are a kind of established religion, albeit a secular one, has been articulated in detail by Rockne McCarthy and his colleagues Gordon Spykman, Donald Oppewal, Walfred Peterson, James W. Skillen, and William A. Harper.[34] These scholars show, by careful analysis of the history, philosophy, and practice of the public schools, that just as the country cannot have an established religion, it likewise cannot afford an established school system with an established philosophy of education. Samuel L. Blumenfeld does an especially good job of documenting the historical origin of the anti-religious bias in our present system—a bias that began with Horace Mann.[35]

The clarity and strength of the positions articulated by Arons, McCarthy, Blumenfeld, and many others make it clear that the period of conflict or strife over education is far from over. In fact, the legal, constitutional, and historical arguments noted here are just beginning to be understood. These are, if you will, young ideas just beginning to spread and have impact. Meanwhile, private schools, especially religious schools, continue to grow. For example, in the fall of 1985 the Reform Jews of America came out in support of religious schools for the first time in their history.[36] In their national convention, this liberal group, long one of the strongest supporters of the public schools, voted by two to one to support private religious schools. They still support public schools as well. But the majority wanted a deeper religious education because they were concerned that their children were being heavily secularized in the public schools. Like many religious Americans, the Reform Jews have come to understand that the state-controlled public school is the major engine of secularism. The result of such education is that children often lose their own religious faith or become vulnerable to recruitment by other religions or by strange cults.

Finally, home schooling is also growing very rapidly in popularity.[37] Thousands of families are pulling their children out of the public schools in order to teach them at home. Such a growth in the disenchantment with public school values and philosophy will not soon be stemmed.

No, the "school wars" are still heating up, and some kind of sensible solution is needed soon lest the schools become even more of a battleground than they are today. The recent lawsuits over school textbooks seem to be pointing in that direction. Should conflict over content in textbooks and in character education grow, then the basic curriculum of the schools is likely to be paralyzed or reduced to some incredibly low, least-common-denominator as the various parties seek to have their position represented and to have offensive statements removed. So again we ask, "What should be done?"

The Particular Solution: Tax Support of Religious and Private Schools

Fortunately, there is a sensible answer to our question, one that already has an excellent track record. Education tax credits and vouchers have been proposed and cogently defended for some years. A well-known case for them is that given by Coons and Sugarman[38] (see also the scholarly discussion in Everhart[39]). Very generally, the arguments for a voucher system or for a system of education tax credit or a child education credit are overwhelmingly convincing. As time goes on, the basic case for tax support will continue to spread as more and more people understand its justice.

It is necessary to articulate here one important kind of rationale expressed in a book by Sister Raymond McLaughlin (1979).[40]

Her basic contention is one that is rarely mentioned but one that needs to become widely appreciated. Very simply, she documents the fact that *every other major Western democracy* except the United States already supports nonpublic (that is, religious) schools with public money. Furthermore, as she documents the history of how this support developed in other countries, she shows that most of the issues that are central to our present school conflicts were fought through in other democracies on their way to reaching very similar solutions—solutions involving tax support for private and religious schools.

The example of Holland is instructive. Very briefly, the history of the Dutch school conflict is as follows. By 1810 or so, the Dutch government had set up state-controlled secular schools which all children were obliged to attend. Catholics and orthodox Protestants were united in their resistance to the state monopoly and their "struggle for freedom and justice in education was to continue for over one hundred years."[41] Catholic and Protestant concerted action was politically effective, and by 1848 an amendment to the Dutch Constitution allowed non-governmental agencies to build, operate, and control their own schools. It was then at least legal for church-related schools to exist. Of course, the costs of these new schools were not covered by the state.

> . . . On the contrary, sponsors of private schools had to build and maintain them out of their own resources. Moreover, they were obliged to pay taxes to build and maintain public schools which, with good conscience, they could not use. The situation for religious-minded parents [1848-1920] was similar to what exists today in the U.S., the only country now among the great Western democracies holding to this outdated view.[42]

However, the Dutch Catholics and Protestants were not satisfied with the injustice of having to pay for their schools and the state schools. Hence the struggle entered a new phase. Catholic and Protestant political parties were formed to represent their viewpoint in Parliament since both faiths were alarmed at the treatment of religion in the state public schools. Finally, the Catholics and Protestants formed a political coalition "united in their views on the necessity of a religious and moral education for their children."[43] (The possibility today of new religious political parties developing in the United States out of a similar conflict is quite real.) In 1887, small sums of government money were allowed for private schools. The pressure from the religious coalition continued to grow, as did the number of Protestant and Catholic schools.

Finally, by 1920, all private schools received financial parity with the state schools. The new policy allowed any private group to establish a school as long as the school met minimum health standards and a minimum student size. Today Dutch schools are run by the state, by Protestant churches, by the Catholic church, and by those devoted to certain philosophies of education such as the Montessori schools. The school wars, which lasted for more than one hundred years, are over in Holland. These wars were in many respects the single most intense issue in Dutch politics for years. However, since 1920, a cooperative atmosphere has reigned among the previously warring parties. In fact, the different schools all cooperate in lobbying the government for financial support. The greater the amount of money for education, the more all the schools benefit.

This Dutch solution was based on certain principles of education now clearly understood and valued by the Dutch. A recent document published by the Netherlands Ministry of Education states:

> ... Freedom to give education fails to achieve its purpose unless it means parents, irrespective of their financial position, are free to choose the education they want for their children. This required that private schools had to have the same rights as public, i.e., state or municipal schools, in the material sense too.... The Dutch public regards it [the educational system] as a prized possession, because it enables every section of the population to give expression in its own way to the spiritual values that it considers of fundamental importance....[44]

The basic principle, of course, behind the system so rightly prized by the Dutch is that "parents must be given the opportunity of providing their children with the education that conforms to their way of life."[45] Only recently have Americans begun to understand this principle; the prominent educator James S. Coleman comes close when he comments: "Perhaps, then, if I dare commit heresy ... the school should not be an agent of the State or the larger society, but an agent of the community of families closest to the child."[46]

Sr. McLaughlin points out that the same kind of war occurred and the same general peace was finally arrived at in England, Scotland, Australia, West Germany, France, and Belgium. Isn't it time the United States achieved such an obviously just solution? This solution has resolved the problem in countries whose religious, legal, and political backgrounds are most similar to ours.

It is also important to point out that our own American history also suggests that the Dutch solution is very likely to work. We have had Catholic schools, Lutheran schools, Jewish schools, Dutch Reform schools, Montessori schools, and many other religious and private schools for years, but they have not resulted in cultural divisions or conflict.

The alternative to tax support for private and religious schools is for America's school wars to escalate still further, to generate still more anger and animosity. As long as this struggle exists, the education of millions of children will suffer, and millions of American taxpayers and parents will continue to protest the present unjust situation. With the broad outlines of the solution so clear from the experience of other countries, it is surely wiser to move toward such an already tested solution of the school problem. Only then will we Americans be able to replace the current conflict with much needed cooperation and much longed for domestic tranquility.

Part of Final Report: NIE-G-84-0012; Project No. 2-0099
Equity in Values Education
Religion in American Textbooks: A Review of the Literature

Dr. Donald Oppewal
Professor of Education
Calvin College
Grand Rapids, Michigan

Introduction

This report focuses on studies that have analyzed the treatment of religion and traditional religious values in elementary and secondary school textbooks. This survey of the literature is supplemented by the author's own research in the same area and will cover a sampling of texts from literature, biology, health, social studies (including civics), and history.

An ERIC search, covering the years 1966-84 and using descriptors like textbook, bias, religious values, and equity, turned up about ten usable pieces of research on specific textbook materials. These sources, plus those already known by the author, and his own textbook research constitute the sources for this report.

It will be assumed that textbooks do treat value-laden matters, whether these be in science, language arts, or social studies. Previous studies of textbook treatment of blacks and women have shown the great difficulty in representing fairly their contributions. For ten or twenty years now the bias of textbooks on these topics has been systematically identified. What this report proposes to do is to apply similar criteria to evaluate the treatment of religion and traditional religious values.

Table 1, designed for detecting "Types of Sex and Ethnic Bias" and drawn up from other sources (Gall, 1981), contains six possible ways in which bias can occur. This report will often use these categories as a screen through which the textbook material will be filtered.

Table 1

Types of Sex and Ethnic Bias

1. Invisibility: Certain groups are underrepresented in curricular materials. The significant omission of women and minority groups has become so great as to imply that these groups are of less value, importance, and significance in our society.

2. Stereotyping: By assigning traditional and rigid roles or attributes to a group, instructional materials stereotype and limit the abilities and potential of that group. Not only are careers stereotyped, but so, too, are intellectual abilities, personality characteristics, physical appearance, social status, and domestic roles. Stereotyping denies students a knowledge of the diversity, complexity, and variation of any group of individuals. Children who see themselves portrayed only in stereotypic ways may internalize those stereotypes and fail to develop their own unique abilities, interests, and full potential.

3. Imbalance/Selectivity: Textbooks perpetuate bias by presenting only one interpretation of an issue, situation, or group of people. This imbalanced account restricts the knowledge of students regarding the varied perspectives which may apply to a particular situation. Through selective presentation of materials, textbooks distort reality and ignore complex and differing viewpoints.

4. Unreality: Textbooks frequently present an unrealistic portrayal of our history and our contemporary life experience. Controversial topics are glossed over and discussions of discrimination and prejudice are avoided. This unrealistic coverage denies children the information they need to recognize, understand, and perhaps some day conquer the problems that plague our society.

5. Fragmentation/Isolation: By separating issues related to minorities and women from the main body of the text, instructional materials imply that these issues are less important than and not part of the dominant culture.

6. Linguistic Bias: Curricular materials reflect the discriminatory nature of our language. Masculine terms and pronouns, ranging from our "forefathers" to the generic "he," deny the participation of women in our society. Further, occupations such as "mailman" are given masculine labels that deny the legitimacy of women working in these fields.

Sources: Shirley McCune and Martha Matthews, eds. *Implementing Title IX and Attaining Sex Equity: A Workshop Package for Postsecondary Educators* (Washington, D.C.: U.S. Government Printing Office, 1978). See also Meredith Gall, *Evaluating and Selecting Curriculum Materials* (Boston: Allyn & Bacon, 1981).

In addition, this report will focus on what alternatives, if any, to traditional religious beliefs are present in textbooks. The *Humanist Manifesto*s will constitute the immediate reference point for identifying if alternatives to theism and traditional religion are expressed in those texts chosen in the various studies reported here.

Summary of a Humanist Creed

While this summary from *Humanist Manifesto I* (1933) and *Humanist Manifesto II* (1973) is the work of the author, a remarkably similar list of six tenets of humanism has been identified by John Whitehead and John Conlan, "The Establishment of the Religion of Secular Humanism and its First Amendment Implications," *Texas Tech Law Review,* 10 (1978).

1. Humanism holds to an evolutionary explanation of both human rights and development.
Manifesto I, second thesis:

Humanism believes that man is a part of nature, and that he has emerged as a result of a continuous process.

Manifesto II, second thesis:

Modern science discredits such historic concepts as the "ghost in the machine" and the "separable soul." Rather, science affirms that the human species is an emergence from natural evolutionary forces. As far as we know, the total personality is a function of the biological organism transacting in a social and cultural context.

2. Humanism believes that the scientific method is applicable to all areas of human concern and is the only means of determining truth.

Manifesto I, fifth thesis:

Religion must formulate its hopes and plans in the light of the scientific spirit and method.

Manifesto II, Preface:

We need to extend the uses of scientific method, not renounce them.

Manifesto II, first thesis:

The controlled use of scientific methods, which have transformed the natural and social sciences since the Renaissance, must be extended further in the solution of human problems.

3. Humanism affirms cultural relativism, the belief that values are grounded only in a given culture and have no transcultural normativity.

Manisfesto I, fifth thesis:

Humanism asserts that the nature of the universe depicted by modern science makes unacceptable any supernatural or cosmic guarantees of human values.

Manifesto II, third thesis:

We affirm that moral values derive their source from human experience. Ethics is autonomous and situational, needing no theological or ideological sanction. Ethics stems from human need and interest.

4. Humanism affirms an anthropocentric and naturalistic view of life.

Manifesto I, eighth thesis:

Religious humanism considers the complete realization of human personality to be the end of man's life and seeks its development and fulfillment in the here and now.

Manifesto I, tenth thesis:

It follows that there will be no uniquely religious emotions and attitudes of the kind hitherto associated with belief in the supernatural.

Manifesto I, fifteenth thesis:

Man is at last becoming aware that he alone is responsible for the realization of the world of his dreams, that he has within himself the power for its achievement.

Manifesto II, first thesis:

We find insufficient evidence for belief in the existence of the supernatural; it is either meaningless or irrelevant to the question of the survival and fulfillment of the human race. As non-theists we begin with humans, not God, nature, not deity. We can discover no divine purpose or providence for the human species. While there is much we do not know, humans are responsible for what we are or will become. No deity will save us; we must save ourselves.

5. Humanism affirms an ethic of individualism, one in which personal values take precedence over community standards for behavior.

Manifesto II, fifth thesis:

The preciousness and dignity of the individual person is a central humanist value. . . . We believe in maximum individual autonomy consonant with social responsibility.

Manifesto II, sixth thesis:

While we do not approve of exploitive, denigrating forms of sexual expression, neither do we wish to prohibit, by law or social sanction, sexual behavior between consenting adults. . . . Short of harming others or compelling them to do likewise, individuals should be permitted to pursue their life styles as they desire.

Manifesto II, seventh thesis:

To enhance freedom and dignity the individual must experience a full range of civil liberties in all societies. . . . It also includes a recognition of an individual's right to die with dignity, euthanasia, and the right to suicide.

6. Humanism affirms cultural determinism, the belief that values in a given society are largely determined by environmental circumstances.

Manifesto I, fourth thesis:

Humanism recognizes that man's religious culture and civilization, as clearly depicted by anthropology and history, are the product of a gradual development due to his interaction with his natural environment and with his social heritage. The individual born into a particular culture is largely molded to that culture.

7. Humanism believes in the innate goodness and perfectibility of the human species.

Manifesto I, fifteenth thesis:

We assert that humanism will: (a) affirm life rather than deny it; (b) seek to elicit possibilities of life, not flee from it; and (c) endeavor to establish the conditions of a satisfactory life for all, not merely for the few. By this positive morale and intention humanism will be guided, and from this perspective and alignment the techniques and efforts of humanism will flow.... Man is at last becoming aware that he alone is responsible for the realization of the world of his dreams, that he has within himself the power for its achievement. He must set intelligence and will to the task.

Manifesto II, Preface:

But views that merely reject theism are not equivalent to humanism. They lack commitment to the positive belief in the possibilities of human progress and the values central to it.... The humanist outlook will tap the creativity of each human being and provide the vision and courage for us to work together. This outlook emphasizes the role human beings can play in their own spheres of action.

Thus the major sections of this report use both Table 1 and the *Humanist Manifesto* as tools to identify to what extent traditional religious values are underrepresented or pejoratively presented.

While no list of these traditional values is possible, what will characterize them as being religious, traditional, or both is that they assume a transcendent or objective anchorage for their vitality and validity. When this transcendent, or religious, dimension of life is underrepresented, in literature for example, then the text can be said to expose the learner to a view of life which does not fairly represent the variety of views present in society. This phenomenon would relate to Table 1, number one, the "Invisibility" criterion, and number three, the "Imbalance/Selectivity" criterion, and number four, the "Unreality" criterion. When, in addition, traditional views are treated pejoratively, the phenomenon would relate to number two, the "Stereotyping" criterion, and number four, the "Unreality" criterion. These four criteria explained in Table 1 will be used to determine whether religious and traditional values and beliefs are accorded equitable treatment in the texts under analysis.

Literature Anthologies

Anthologies for literature class are used extensively in upper elementary and secondary school English classes. Because they draw from a vast pool of available material, editorial judgment as to what is appropriate for a given grade level enters heavily into the selection. Some are organized or sequenced historically and others are grouped into genres or by themes, and this may also affect editorial judgment about what literary materials will be selected.

The underrepresentation criterion and the pejorative evidence criterion (see Table 1) will be used singly or together in examining selected texts. Since no statistical reference point exists for the amount of attention that *should* be given to religious or traditional values, the best that can be done is to document the amount. However, some evidence exists that over the last twenty-five years the amount of attention given to theistic beliefs and practices has significantly diminished. One study of Missouri textbooks in the early fifties (Pflug, 1955) concluded that even thirty years ago:

> The closer we get in textbook descriptions of present day life and literature the fewer theistic references there are. There is a noticeable tapering-off of religious references in the modern period. Thus an alert student may feel that the textbook dealing with today's problems no longer cites religion as a molding force in society. (p. 260)

Another study (McCarthy, et al., 1981, p. 122) involved a comparison of two junior high literature anthologies published by the same company twenty-five years apart. The research methodology consisted of counting the number of lines, in either editorial comment or the literary content, which recognized a religious transcendent dimension of life. Inclusion of the religious dimension of life was identified as consisting of any of the following:

1. devotional religious acts described, such as praying, Bible reading, church-going, hymn singing
2. religious occupations depicted, such as ministers or elders of churches, missionaries, or church school teachers
3. moral decisions made in an explicitly religious context and using religious sanctions.

The number of lines containing any of the above was then calculated as a percentage of the total lines in the text. It was determined that three times as much attention was devoted to this dimension in the earlier edition. The actual percentages were: 1.3% in the earlier edition and .45% in the edition published twenty-five years later.

The Kanawha County, West Virginia, textbook controversy in the early seventies provided the setting for another textbook analysis by scholars. Two scholars (Hillocks, 1978; McNearney, 1975), working independently, concluded that at bottom the conflict was ideological and that it was between traditional theism and some form of humanism. George Hillocks is a University of Chicago professor of education and expert in language arts. He did an analysis of the language arts textbooks that precipitated the controversy. His analysis revealed that only six of the thirty-eight prose selections mentioned Christians or Christian beliefs. In addition, he noted that *all* of the six prose selections were "pejorative of Christianity, either directly in adverse comments about the shortcomings of Christianity or indirectly by showing Christians as hypocrites or fools" (p. 646). He also noted that only seven of forty-six poems in a given text dealt with matters in the Christian tradition (p. 642). It would seem that there is, in this sampling, both a limited treatment and a pejorative depiction of traditional religious values. These would then fail the two criteria drawn from Table 1.

Further personal research by the author has focused on textbooks published in the 1970s. Those anthologies which reach back in to the seventeenth and eighteenth centuries for their materials tend to score higher in terms of attention to the religious or transcendent dimension of life. This would be because of the inclusion of writers like Jonathan Edwards and Nathaniel Hawthorne, who persistently provide lines fitting the three categories of devotional acts, characters in religious occupations, and moral decisions calling upon religious sanctions. One such text (McFarland, 1972) includes not only these writers but also the twentieth century Arthur Miller play *The Crucible*, in which the setting is an early New England colony. Even with these writers included, the total number of lines in this text is 2% of the total. Since editorial comment is sketchy and no teacher's manual is provided, there is no available evidence to determine whether the class discussion treatment is pejorative or supportive of the ideas and practices, although the play *The Crucible* could hardly be said to be a sympathetic treatment of Puritan society. No recent literary material of a positive or serious kind with respect to traditional religion is included.

Another type of anthology, arranging literature according to genres or types of literature, presents a different set of editorial judgments in the selection of the content. One text (Gordon, 1975) chosen for scrutiny includes an extensive section on "Myths, Fables, and Legends." Since this genre deals almost exclusively with gods and other super-human beings and events, a large number of lines are devoted to descriptions of beliefs about the transcendent. When the extensive mythology section is included, the percentage of lines devoted to exposure to this phenomenon is 23%. Without the inclusion of this section it is 1%. The company provides as supplement to the student text a *Handbook and Key* by B. Welch. Analysis revealed about the same percentages as in the student text.

If one were sensitive in this case to the possible pejorative treatment of traditional religious beliefs and values, it would not be evident in the number of lines of religious material. It would lie in the editorial judgment that Judeo-Christian literature, particularly Bible events, were grouped along with Greek and other myths and fables. While other myths and fables are accepted as fictional interpretations of human origins and morals, the Old Testament in religious orthodoxy is presented as historical event, not literary fabrication. The comparison in the *Teacher Guide* (pp. 164-174) between biblical myths and other myths in explaining human beings seems to ignore this key difference and is clearly biased against the traditional belief as to the historicity of the biblical narrative.

One noteworthy quote from the student text (p. XVIII) strongly suggests the human origin of all myths:

Man has always wanted to know how the earth was created, why there are seasons, why there are storms, why there is misery, what the limits are of his power and knowledge. To answer these great questions about himself and the universe he has fashioned superhumans or gods.

In summary, the literature texts examined do contain material which exposes the student to traditional religious values, with amounts varying from negligible to significant, depending upon whether the texts contain writings from earlier periods. Pejorative treatment of Judeo-Christian values and interpretations was the result of underrepresenting religious views and according biblical materials, when presented, the status of literature—no more normative than any other literary expression.

Health/Sex Education Textbooks

This curriculum area, distinguishable broadly from science and narrowly from biology, is one in which the teaching materials are very value-laden. They typically (Bucher, 1981) deal with nutrition, tobacco, alcohol and other drugs, diseases, and even sometimes first aid (for burns and poisons, for example). The sex education component surfaces under such rubrics as "reproductive systems" or "venereal diseases."

Nutrition as a topic deals with diet, including the traditional four basic food groups. The value dimension appears again and again, in spite of the statement to the teacher in the "Philosophy" section (p. T3) that "the purpose of this text is to provide students with factual information concerning the mental, physical, and social aspects of health" and then adds the criterion "the scientific basis for intelligent self-help preventive medicine." An example of the violation of this principle is in the treatment of controversial issues such as vegetarianism. Using the expression "many people," the advantages given are that it is less expensive, less wasteful, and healthier, and concludes that "a vegetarian diet can be very healthful, especially if it permits the use of dairy products and eggs" (p. 162). Directly germane to this study is the single sentence assertion that "some people adopt this diet for religious reasons." This token acknowledgment of the relevance of religious belief is not supported, as the other arguments are, by any explanatory material. Thus the power of religion is underrepresented, compared to other arguments.

Another text (LaPlace, 1980) for secondary health class is a more striking example of value-laden material. A comparison of two chapters will reveal the negative and positive treatment of topics. Chapter nine, "Tobacco," is heavily loaded against smoking, linking it aggressively, in over fifteen pages, with cancer and heart disease. It ends its treatment with "What to Do About Smoking" and the direct admonition that smokers "must admit that they *can* and *should* quit" (p. 271).

By contrast, chapter six, "Sexual Behavior," has a consistent tone of approval for a wide variety of sexual behaviors. Three kinds of arguments are used to support them:

1. Use of statistics which show frequency of some behavior, like homosexuality (p. 182), masturbation (p. 177), and premarital intercourse (p. 179).

2. Use of the phrases "experts say" or "most authorities agree" as a means to lend support to these behaviors.

3. The pitting of *tradition* against *now*, with tradition always shown in an unfavorable light. A striking example of this is the bold assertion that "although homosexual acts have traditionally been categorized as deviant or unnatural, there is no evidence that they are any more or less so than heterosexual acts" (p. 182).

A strong prejudice against religious and traditional values is evident in the exclusive use of the above criteria. The argument from statistics or frequence of occurrence ignores the religious value dimension as normative and would be used nowhere else to legitimize an act, such as lying or stealing. The "experts say" argument is biased because the experts are self-selected and usually the most liberal. The argument which pits the present against past tradition assumes that newer views are more right or socially better. All three criteria are consistent with moral relativism and are much more than simply information.

Another text (Pengalley, 1974), designed for college level, is an even more striking example of the condemnation of religious sanctions and approval of the frequency criterion. In the treatment of incest and homosexuality, the following is inserted:

> Unfortunately, we are inevitably on dangerous ground when discussing sexual behavior because the civil laws governing it are nearly always based on religious dogma, taboos, and superstition, which in turn are compounded by plain ignorance. (p. 138)

This follows a specific value statement on incest in which approval is indicated by the assertion that incest:

> perhaps the most universally condemned sexual behavior of all, was considered highly desirable by the ancient Egyptian pharaohs. Indeed, Cleopatra was the last of a long line of brother-sister matings, and from all accounts she was no insignificant woman. (p. 138)

The frequency of occurrence criterion is used to provide support for what have been traditionally called *deviant* and not merely variant sexual behaviors. In a section entitled "Forms of Variant Sexual Behavior" (pp. 141-155), homosexuality is shown to be present in a long list of animals, including fish, birds, lizards, and mammals like the cow. The generalization is made that "so far as mammals are concerned, it is safe to say that in all species that have been studied homosexual activity has been observed and is indeed common" (p. 141). When applied to human behavior, the criterion is exhibited when it states that "so far as the incidence of homosexuality is concerned, Kinsey estimated that 37% of American males have had some form of homosexual experience during their lives, and that 5% have been exclusively homosexual during their entire lives" (p. 142).

The frequency argument is also used to assess affirmatively sadism and masochism in the following:

> In any case, both sadism and masochism are widespread; as with so many forms of sexual behavior, the seeds are within all of us. Indeed, millions of sexual partners engage in minor sadistic rituals as routine before sexual intercourse. (p. 148)

An extensive treatment of pornography combines the frequency criterion—"there is probably not a single man, woman, or child who has not had at least some exposure to pornography" (p. 155)—with the appeal to selected experts, and concludes that "all the evidence we have indicates that parents and society worry quite unnecessarily about the effects of pornography, particularly on children" (p. 155). When treating the matter of sexual relations before marriage, the author pits tradition against the frequency criterion, using the latter to discredit tradition, as in the following:

> In any case, traditional sexual morality simply no longer has much meaning for the young, for recent surveys show that one-half of all females and two-thirds of males experience sexual intercourse before marriage. (p. 71)

Negative treatment of religious orthodoxy is revealed in this text in two additional ways. One is by a case history in which "the adverse effects of religious orthodoxy on sexual functioning in general" (p. 114) are depicted in detail, with pejorative comments that in the given case the partners were "trained by theological demand to uninformed immaturity in matters of sexual connotation . . ." (p. 115). The case study ends with the comment that "the serious damage caused by various religious indoctrinations to any form of natural sex behavior seems too obvious to warrant elaboration" (p. 116). Another case history is detailed with the same language (p. 122).

The second form of negative treatment of the role of religious belief occurs in chapter thirteen, "Cross-cultural and Historical Aspects of Sexual Behavior." The past is divided into two types of societies: sexually restrictive and sexually permissive. The sexually permissive societies, usually primitive island societies, are described affirmatively; sexually restrictive societies are shown to be those infected by religious beliefs, as shown by the assertion of "the severe inhibitory influences exerted by Roman Catholic and Protestant churches alike, including some newer 'home grown' ones" (p. 242).

In summary, the examination of these three textbooks on health/sex education reveals the consistent taking of sides on controversial matters. Both religious beliefs and traditional morality, when recognized as relevant to the subject, are pejoratively pitted against three substitutes for the transcendent norms claimed in traditional morality. These three substitutes are statistics (frequency criterion) as determining the norm for human behavior; the authority of narrowly selected experts; and the consistent assumption that newer and more recent opinion is superior to earlier and traditional beliefs. Taken collectively, these three criteria reveal that traditional and religious values receive a seriously unfair and unbalanced treatment in these textbooks on health and sex education.

Secondary Biology Textbooks

The BSCS (Biological Science Curriculum Study) texts, four in number, offer a striking example of how values are taught: (1) by positions taken on controversial social issues arising out of biology (like drugs, the population explosion, human reproduction) and (2) by the basic, life-orientation ideology which undergirds the treatment. When presented in a textbook, social issues can never be merely described; they are also interpreted as to their seriousness by what value judgments are made and by what authorities are given as reference points. In all of these interpretive descriptions the author's ideology is expressed but not named.

The BSCS series represents a recent aggressive attempt to make biology relevant to learners by insertion of social issues into the discipline (James, 1974; Kieffer, 1975; Sonneborn, 1972). One study identified eleven "controversial issues and biosocial problems" present in varying degrees in BSCS textbooks (Leven and Lindbeck, 1979). The authors found that all presented some of the issues, but no one presented all. What is notable in Leven and Lindbeck's analysis is the almost total absence of recognition that religious beliefs bear directly on the issues being discussed.

In a different study (McCarthy, et al., 1981) the four BSCS books were also analyzed for bias. (The four textbooks are *Biological Science: Molecules to Man,* 3rd ed. [Houghton Mifflin Co., 1976]; *Biological Science: An Inquiry Into Life,* 3rd ed. [Harcourt Brace Jovanovich, 1973]; *Biological Science: An Ecological Approach* [Rand McNally Co., 1973]; *Modern Biology* [Holt, Rinehart & Winston, 1977.]) While each of the four was published by a different company, all were written under grants from The National Science Foundation with funds appropriated by Congress. They are reputedly used by more than 50% of American high school students studying biology (Hurd, 1976). Analysis of state adoptions revealed that of the twenty-one states requiring an agency recommendation, nine states have approved two of the books, eleven states have approved a third, and twelve have approved a fourth (McCarthy, 1981, p. 125).

The combination of their tax dollar funding, their development by a quasi-governmental agency, and their widespread official adoption and use gives this group of texts a power not accorded many school textbooks.

In analyzing these books, the research methodology consisted of summarizing the tenets identified in *Humanist Manifesto I* (1933) and *Humanist Manifesto II* (1973). The texts were examined for the degree of congruence between these tenets and the perspectives which they presented. Hundreds of passages in all four demonstrate that the books express several key theses: (1) the origin of the universe through natural processes; (2) the naturalistic development of life from nonlife; (3) the evolution of present living forms through mutation and natural selection; and (4) the evolution of human beings from an ancestry common with apes (Bird, 1978). These theses contradict traditional religious belief on these points. Both the aggressive explicating of these beliefs and the ignoring of the alternative beliefs represent a bias against traditional religious beliefs and for the viewpoint of secular humanism as expressed in the *Humanist Manifesto*s. One summary doctrine in the *Manifesto*s is that "humanism holds to an evolutionary explanation of human origins and development," while another is that "humanism believes that the scientific method is applicable to all areas of human concerns, and is the only valid means of determining truth." There is a high degree of congruence between these *Manifesto* beliefs and the implicit and explicit teachings of these books. When authors incorporate into their texts views on the nature and destiny of man, and not just the biological data, then they may be said to be ideologically biased. When the bias is identified with secular humanism, then one may conclude that the views are hostile to traditional religious beliefs in these same areas. The bias is more basic than simply underrepresentation of traditional views; it is the explicit teaching of views which are hostile to them.

In summary, these four texts in secondary biology seem to have shifted from the traditional focus on biological concepts to controversial socio-moral issues. In so doing, the possibility of exhibiting bias is increased. In this sample the result has been that traditional grounding of values has not only been underrepresented but almost totally replaced by the values sanctioned by secular humanism.

Civics/Government Text

This curriculum area is a required course in either junior or senior high in most schools; the textbook selected (*American Political Behavior*, 1972) has been identified as one of the two current front-runners in sales (Le Fever, 1978). It appears on the adoption list of eight of twenty-one states having such procedures (McCarthy, et al., 1981, p. 126).

The McCarthy study found a striking and explicit similarity between the creed of humanism and the viewpoint of this text. It is illustrated by the humanist doctrine, which says that the scientific method is applicable to all areas of human concern and is the only valid means for determining truth. Both in the *Teacher's Guide* and the main text, this view is explicitly underscored. The *Guide* says that one of the most important goals established for the text is "influencing students to value scientific approaches to the verification of factual claims and rational analysis of value claims" (p. 2). While admitting to some limitations of the scientific method, "social scientists feel that by emulating the scientific method to the greatest possible degree, they can uncover more of the regularities of human behavior than have previously been set forth" (p. 11).

In the student text, the commitment is made even more explicit in the following:

> Scientific inquiry is the best method we have for making decisions about competing alternative hypotheses about reality. It is the best method, because it is the most useful and reliable. (p. 56)

This is a close paraphrase of humanist doctrine two and contrasts sharply with the religious and many other disciplines' views on the sources of moral truth.

This explicit commitment leads consistently to several other key beliefs of humanism. Doctrine four is that humanism affirms an anthropocentric and naturalistic view of life. This is evident from the way the authors treat other nonscientific approaches to understanding political behavior, one of which is called "the method of revelation." It is judged to be inadequate because:

> There is no easy way to confirm the claims of those who have experienced revelations. Ultimately, one must accept the word of the prophet on faith or reject his statements. (p. 55)

The authors state that they are not opposed to religion, its beliefs, or values. Indeed they point out that many scientists are religious people who attend church (p. 53). However, as the previous passages show, revelation claims do not stand up to the test of their understanding of the scientific method and are thus quietly discounted.

One looks in vain in the text for any serious treatment of the institution of the church and its role in society. Ignoring the church does not seem to be an oversight but rather a conscious decision to discount the claim that the church offers a normative vision of life that has a bearing on social life and political principles. The claim of the church to a normative vision of life that has a bearing on society is openly discredited in the section entitled "Beliefs Based on Faith." Here the text says, "A belief based on faith cannot be tested scientifically, since it cannot be confirmed or rejected in terms of what exists" (p. 53).

The irrelevance of religious beliefs and the role of the organized church in political events is particularly striking in the treatment of the Montgomery, Alabama, bus boycott of 1955-56 (pp. 132-139). In a generally sympathetic treatment of the black cause, the text tells the story of how segregation was fought and eventually defeated. The fact that Martin Luther King, Jr. was a pastor and that the black churches played a key role is ignored. Political power and efficient organization are identified as the key factors. Thus the irrelevance of organized religion and theism are effectively taught by ignoring the church's impact on a political struggle in a very specific instance. At best such a representation of Martin Luther King, Jr.'s life and actions is a serious distortion of the truth.

A different, but related, perspective of the text relates to doctrine three, which states that humanism affirms cultural relativism, the belief that values are grounded only in a given culture and have no trans-cultural normativity. This view appears in both explicit statements and in the book's overall treatment of various dissident groups in American politics. A general explanation of how values are grounded is provided:

> Through the process of socialization, an individual learns what is considered right and wrong political behavior in his society. Through socialization an infant born in the United States of America learns to behave politically in the American way. (p. 101)

Whether in a description of the Amish (pp. 91-99), the poor blacks in the Alabama bus boycott (pp. 132-138), the antiwar demonstrators (pp. 129-131, 155-158), or other groups, the beliefs, values, and priorities of any group are shown to stem essentially from the cultural conditioning of the group. Thus the student is taught that values are culturally bound. This contrasts sharply with the traditional religious belief that there are value norms which transcend any given culture.

The evidence suggests that this civics/government text does indeed exhibit bias—one that goes deep into politics and covers fundamental ways of looking at society and its institutions. By both underrepresentation of the role of religious belief and the church in society and the negative treatment of the grounding of religious belief, this text clearly fails the test of equity and fairness.

History Texts

Most states require a course in American history before a student graduates from high school, so all students receive some formal instruction in at least one period of history. The American history text selected (Todd and Curti, 1972) has been approved by ten of the twenty-one states having adoption policies. Estimated sales figures reveal that the text sold 200,000 copies in 1977 alone. It is therefore a widely adopted and respected text—and one that, according to one study, unabashedly states its perspective (McCarthy, 1981).

Humanist doctrine one states that humanism believes in an evolutionary explanation of both human origins and development. While this book does not address the question of human origins, it does perpetuate notions of evolutionary development by stressing adaptation to an environment and natural selection. For instance, in the sections on American colonization (pp. 54-96), the authors consistently point out that the settlers had to change their manners, language, techniques, and values, for the new environment demanded radically new emphases and techniques in the lives of the colonists. Either the colonists had to meet the challenges of the frontier or suffer dire consequences. Although undisguised and explicit passages revealing this are not abundant, the book consistently uses the evolutionary model of change and adaptation to a new environment to explain the failures and successes of various leaders and movements, and it largely ignores the role of religious belief in shaping that adaptation.

The text also has a strong commitment to the scientific method, not only as a valid means for determining truth in history but also as the only reliable method with which to understand all areas of human concern. First, the authors believe in using the scientific method in the writing of history. The student is told:

> Like the social scientist, the historian uses the scientific mode of inquiry in making his investigation. . . . In subjecting their sources of evidence to "the most severe and detailed tests possible," historians use scientific modes of inquiry . . . .(pp. 206-207)

Second, the authors favorably portray the advancement of the scientific method in American culture. For instance, the authors highlight the scientific method as it was applied to medicine, agriculture, and chemistry (pp. 556-559, 810-817). Another example of eulogizing the scientific method is near the end of the book:

... by the 1970s the United States and other technologically advanced nations had the capability—or could acquire the capability—of doing just about anything men wanted to do. Stated concisely, through science and technology men had acquired Godlike powers. (p. 822)

Finally, the authors assent to the application of the scientific method to other areas of life. One of the stiking features of this text is a series of essays, interspersed throughout the book, explaining the nature, methodology, and concepts of selected social science disciplines. Case studies in these areas are also provided that demonstrate how the findings of these investigations can aid us in understanding the issues and periods of American history. The authors emphasize that the scientific method is a common component of all these disciplines. For example, in the essay on "Sociology" the authors write:

These are the scientific methods of inquiry developed and refined by sociologists.... The social sciences, then, although they differ greatly in the questions they ask, do not differ greatly in their methods of investigation. (p. 94)

In their defense, the authors might contend that they are merely attempting empirically to describe the present state of affairs in the social sciences and history. However, by highlighting and emphasizing the exclusive use of the scientific method in all areas of life, without paying due attention to other methods of determining truth, they are exposing a profound bias in their presentation. Their stance is therefore an epistemological commitment and not merely a commitment to scholarly accuracy.

Another tenet of naturalistic humanism is the belief that values are grounded only in a given culture and are not normative in another culture (doctrine three). Such cultural relativism agrees with several points made in this text, especially in the sections dealing with the colonization of America. The authors discuss how much the values of the pioneers changed in their new environment; that this happened is understandable and plausible. However, the authors go a step further and suggest that all values are relative to a given culture (p. 93).

Another principle of naturalistic humanism is the affirmation of an anthropocentric and naturalistic view of life (doctrine four). In various subtle and perhaps unwitting ways, the text concurs with this creedal statement, as the following excerpts illustrate. Viewing history as "the record of mankind on earth" (p. 1), the authors describe "the freedoms we cherish, the material comforts we enjoy, and the institutions that serve us" as the products of man (*Teacher's Manual*, p. 2). The history of America is regarded as "the most dramatic and significant story in all human history" (p. 6). The Constitution is regarded as "the supreme law" (p. 189). In reflecting on the bicentennial, Americans should celebrate that:

> . . . through understanding and through participation in the democratic political process, they have been able to solve their problems. (p. 843)

This statement is, among other things, simply very bad history since the Civil War represented a major failure of democracy to solve a national problem. Indeed, the Civil War was in many respects a conflict over values so discrepant that physical violence was the only answer. In the preface to the *Teacher's Manual*, the authors express their statement of purpose:

> But if we can help our students to face these problems courageously, intelligently and with humility, we may hope that they will create a richer and more meaningful life for themselves and future generations. (p. 1)

Man is always at the center of the picture the authors paint. What this picture reveals is more than just an absence of transcendent norms or the Christian religion. It asserts an optimistic faith in the ability of man both to create and shape the world he lives in and to solve his own problems. Like the adherents of naturalistic humanism, the authors seem to believe that man is autonomous.

Another very recent study (Bryan, n.d.) surveyed twenty American history texts approved for use in the Montgomery County, Maryland, school system. The results of that study are given in great detail. The author selected some texts for limited approval, but most were criticized for their treatment of the role of religion and religious figures in America. Subtitled "How Public School Textbooks Treat Religion," the study by an ecclesiastical historian found these representative texts to be a mixture of anachronism, discontinuity, and oversimplification (p. 6) in most of their treatment of religion.

Of several significant conclusions in this report, one is that "there is a remarkable consensus to the effect that, after 1700, Christianity has no historical presence in America" (p. 3). Another conclusion is that in representing Puritan ideas and Puritan institutions, "almost every reference to Puritanism is negative" (p. 4). The study also found that later religious and ecclesiastical developments (like the Great Awakening) and their influence on social issues (such as abolition, immigration, women's suffrage, and temperance) are either ignored or misrepresented (pp. 11-12).

Thus, this sampling of American history textbooks reveals that by both historical criteria and pedagogical principles, they underrepresent traditional beliefs or treat them pejoratively.

Elementary Social Studies Texts

Social studies covers a wide range of subject matter dealing with people interacting with each other and their environment. Because its focus is on persons and their social institutions, many value-related questions must be treated, whether in our culture or some other. Some are: Where does the civil government get its authority? What is the family structure like? What role does the church and religion play in the lives of people?

One recent text (Cangemi, 1983) was analyzed for the amount of attention given to the religious dimension of life, classifying such treatment into the incidence of (1) mention of devotional religious acts, (2) depiction of persons with an ecclesiastical identity, and (3) moral issues portrayed as influenced by religion. Since this text is a world culture text, it discusses many societies—ancient, medieval, and modern. In each culture the role of religion, its rituals and its beliefs about ethical matters as well as the afterlife, is described, usually in purely descriptive terms. Only occasionally are the cultures evaluated negatively, such as when the caste system related to the Hindu religion is called "cruel" (p. 261). Religious leaders, like Gandhi, Confucius, Muhammed, and Joan of Arc, are given positive identification.

A striking exception is the final chapter on the United States, treated in twenty pages. References to religious institutions and leaders are nonexistent. The only reference occurs in the simple assertion: "Americans are free to worship as they please" (p. 424). Also, the chapter on "The Soviet Union" has not a single line which would state the role of religion in its culture.

While the total percentage of lines exhibiting a religious dimension in the student text is .029, the *Teacher's Edition* and the editorial materials, consisting of "Section Review" questions, contain even less. No mention of religion occurs in any of the review or discussion questions provided at the end of each chapter, thus suggesting to both student and teacher its insignificance in understanding each society.

In summary, this textbook for upper elementary students includes references to religion in most, but not all, chapters, but neither the teacher nor the student is given encouragement to react to or discuss such influence. The underrepresentation criterion would be most evident in the chapters on the United States and Russia.

Analysis of another secondary social studies text by Weitzman and Gross (1974) reveals a greater degree of similarity in the student text and the instructor's guide than the one just described. The percentage of lines devoted to the religious dimension is 7% in the student text and 4% in the *Teacher's Edition*. The religious dimension in the text is often tied to the art, drama, marriage customs, and holidays of a culture. The description is often sympathetic. The manual for the teacher has, for example, the objective:

> Students should be able to respond with understanding and empathy to the myths and creation stories of historical and living peoples and then to the values inherent in these stories. (p. 10)

Chapter two, "From Angel to Ape," contains material on the conflict between religious and scientific beliefs about human origin and development. The attempt to remain neutral is expressed in the *Guide* by the objective that the student should be able to:

> Characterize religious and scientific explanations of creation and understand the values of each in human societies. (p. 11)

Thus in general this text is neutral, and sometimes sympathetic, toward beliefs about origins derived from religion, although it typically underrepresents traditional religious beliefs.

A way in which this text is subtly pejorative in its treatment of religion is by associating it with myth, ignorance, and early primitive cultures, rather than with sophisticated contemporary thinkers in America and the West. Religion and the values derived from it are depicted as an historical phenomenon, powerful in early cultures but not a living alternative for today.

One of the most controversial of the numerous elementary school textbook series is *Man: A Course of Study* (MACOS), designed for fifth grade. The series contains a wide array of teacher's manuals, student texts, student activity sheets, records, films, maps, and simulation games. It was produced in the mid-1960s under a grant from the National Science Foundation, which in turn is funded by congressional appropriations. The series is reported to have cost over seven million tax dollars for its development and marketing (Marshner, 1975). Like the BSCS biology texts, the series thus can be said to represent a more official ideology than any published by private publishers.

Analysis of state adoptions (McCarthy, 1981) reveals that only one state, California, includes MACOS on its approved list, a low number probably because of the series' controversial qualities. Objections to the materials are many and varied, and not all are relevant for this study. The charges most relevant to our study are that it aggressively teaches both cultural relativism (humanist doctrine three) and environmental determinism (humanist doctrine six). Much of the controversy centers on the unit dealing with Netsilik Eskimos, the only unit dealing with humans. It is also the longest of the units. It is preceded by units dealing with the king salmon, the herring gull, and the baboon, in that order. One might wonder why units dealing with animals dominate in a social studies program named *Man: A Course in Study*, but what all the units have in common is a focus on mating habits, infant rearing practices, and family structure in both animal and human social groupings, in order from simple to complex.

There is considerable evidence in both student and teacher materials that MACOS teaches ethical and cultural relativism. Doctrine three holds that values are grounded within a culture and have no transcultural normativity. Since the student materials are so varied, their ideological outlook is not readily apparent on the surface. However, a number of social practices in the Eskimo unit, such as cannibalism, wife-sharing, and senilicide (abandonment of the aged), are consistently portrayed as plausible and natural responses to the social situation. The student materials do not contain any negative evaluation but merely describe these practices. However, the materials for teachers reveal a clearer ideological orientation. A separate publication, *Talks to Teacher* (Dow, 1970), contains explicit observations that signal congruence between the orientation of MACOS and the sectarian and creedal formulation of humanism on ethical relativism. The project director states as a major objective:

> Second, we hope that through this course children will come to understand that what we regard as acceptable behavior is a product of our culture. (Dow, p. 6)

Elsewhere (Dow, 1975) the director has been even more explicit about whether values are transcultural. In describing one of the overall effects of the materials he says:

For one thing, it questions the notion that there are "eternal truths" about humanity that must be passed down from one generation to the next. (p. 80)

The MACOS series conveys the message of humanist doctrine six, that humanism affirms cultural determinism.

When elements of the humanist doctrines of evolution, cultural relativism, and cultural determinism are present as shapers of curricular materials produced by a quasi-governmental agency, one may well ask whether MACOS does not indeed teach a civic religion which opposes traditional theistic positions on the same issues.

In summary, these texts in social studies would underrepresent religion as a living force today and are pejorative in such under-representation, even when neutrally described. The third, the MACOS materials, reveals most clearly the ideology of humanism as the perspective which is offered as the alternative to traditional religion and its values.

School Prayers in the Literature Class
Bryce Christensen (Associate Editor of
Chronicles: A Magazine of
American Culture.
[Rockford Institute, Rockford: Illinois])

THOUGH FEW SEEM TO HAVE NOTICED, prayer continues to be a routine part of the public school curriculum, untouched by the Supreme Court's opinions or by most parents' religious convictions. These prayers are the literary prayers offered in the mandatory literature class. Such prayers include Tess of the D'Urberville's desperate but unavailing prayer for the life of her baby, Holden Caulfield's abortive attempt to pray in bed, and the Newspaper Correspondent's fervent petition to the deaf gods of the sea in Crane's "Open Boat." Students may not be forced to *listen* to prayer every morning, but they are often compelled to *study* prayers in their literature class, and the nature of this compulsory prayer is deeply disturbing.

Indeed, most of the literary prayers now studied at taxpayer expense are like the three just cited: ineffectual, incomplete, or ironic. Similarly, most of the literary sermons now mandated in public schools are at odds with religious faith: E.E. Cummings's repudiation of the Resurrection in "O Sweet Spontaneous," Hemingway's machismo nihilism in *The Sun Also Rises,* or Conrad's dubious comparison of paganism and Christianity in *Heart of Darkness,* for instance.

The effects of such prayers and sermons are to be found not only in spiral-bound notebooks but in juvenile sensibilities as well. As a teacher of literature on the secondary and college levels, I have often seen young people whose religious attitudes bear the marks of a public literature course. "I believed in God," wrote one of my freshman students in an essay, "until my high school English teacher helped me become smarter." The irony was that, according to the same essay, his parents (whose taxes paid his teacher) had tried to raise him as a believing church-goer. "Depressing! Depressing! Depressing!" was how a young lady whose Christian faith survived the experience described her forced march in high school through one gloomy atheistic work of literature after another. Another young man reported that his high school English teacher taught him that the only standards to which he was accountable were those of his own making. Yet another young woman reported that the naturalistic literature which she was assigned in public secondary school made her "feel suicidal."

The study of literature hardly need be destructive of religious commitment. From *The Pearl* in Old English to the lyrics of Gerard Manley Hopkins, from *Pilgrim's Progress* to Walker Percy's *Love in the Ruins,* from *The Second Shepherd's Play* to T.S. Eliot's *Murder in the Cathedral,* literature is filled with affirmations of Judeo-Christian faith. Such affirmative works, however, are now little used in most high school literature courses. They are judged "too religious."

But the notion that literature or literary study can avoid being religious is quite new and utterly false. Great poets, playwrights, and novelists must address such questions as the meaning of life, the nature of man, and the role of God in human affairs. Any serious response to these questions is necessarily an affirmation, modification, or repudiation of religious responses as taught in Scripture and within America's various Christian and Jewish communities.

It is not difficult to see, for example, that for a teacher to require public school students to read Bunyan's militantly Protestant *Grace Abounding,* Flannery O'Connor's intensely Christian fiction, or John Dryden's poetic apologia for his conversion to Catholicism, *The Hind and the Panther,* is to make a tax-supported religious statement. But deliberately and systematically to exclude such accomplished literature from the classroom in favor of literary attacks upon scriptural beliefs by such writers as Theodore Drieser, John Steinbeck, or A.E. Housman is just as surely to adopt a tax-subsidized religious position, though one antithetical to most of those paying the tax.

The choice of critical approaches to be fostered, or even permitted, can be as religiously sensitive as the choice of poems and novels. A teacher may, for instance, publicly second G.K. Chesterton's Christian judgment that Hardy's atheistic fatalism made his fiction a dismal joke, or he may cast his lot with the agnostic Ifor Evans in praising Hardy for the "sincerity and courage" of his bleak vision.[1] The teacher may join William Empson in attacking Milton for celebrating allegedly outmoded Christian belief in *Paradise Lost* (in the unlikely event that this text is still used in high school), or she may endorse C.S. Lewis's praise for Milton's celebration of timeless subject.[2] In any event, it is virtually impossible to study literature without making some religious statement.

Current judicial wisdom is that literature of "description" is appropriate for public schools but literature of "devotion" is not. Poets and novelists may describe prayer in their work but may not actually pray. But the distinction between devotion and description is a dubious one. As the poet Wallace Stevens correctly observed, "We live in the description of a place and not in the place itself."[3] In other words, "It is in a description that we live and move and have our being." Whether we will even choose to pray at all depends upon whether our description of the universe, our *Weltanschauung,* includes someone to whom to pray. And the way young teenagers describe their world can be potently influenced by the literature they are required to study.

Certainly, many of the most profound critics of literature have recognized its religious implications. Plato believed that the only poems that should be allowed within his ideal Republic were "hymns to the gods" and panegyrics to pious and heroic men.[4] Samuel Johnson similarly believed that good poets were only those who employed "every idea ... for the enforcement or decoration of moral or religious truth."[5] A century after Johnson, Leo Tolstoy reviewed Plato's reasons for excluding profane poets from his realm and reached this conclusion:

> The estimation of the value of art (i.e., of the feelings it transmits) depends on men's perception of the meaning of life, depends on what they consider to be the good and the evil of life. And what is good and what is evil is defined by what are termed religions.[6]

In our own century, Tolstoy's insight has been reaffirmed by several critics, most notably perhaps by T. S. Eliot. "Literary criticism," Eliot believed, "should be completed by criticism from a definite ethical and theological standpoint."[7]

Just *whose* ethical and theological standpoint should receive tax support for completing criticism in America's literature classes? This is a knotty question and one that legislators and the courts have largely ignored. But as things now stand, skeptical literature teachers routinely use their classrooms as forums for discrediting the beliefs of Christian and Jewish taxpayers. This is costly academic freedom.

The attack in public literature courses upon traditional religious beliefs has become especially pronounced during the last two decades, as devotion has become increasingly unfashionable among America's literary elite, including those who train English teachers and edit literary anthologies. Writing in 1963, Flannery O'Connor complained in an essay entitled "Total Effect and the Eighth Grade" that public school teachers often drag fourteen- and fifteen-year-olds into the world of modern literature before they were prepared by studying more traditional works. Symptomatic of the moral problems this poses, Miss

O'Connor noted, was that while in the Bible or in *Anna Karenina* "adultery is considered a sin," in modern fiction it is "at most, an inconvenience."[8] Writing in 1968, the distinguished literary historian Robert E. Spiller summed up the dominant message of modern literature, drawn primarily from Darwin, Freud, and Marx, as "the confrontation of the individual will by an inexorable and mechanistic Fate."[9]

It is not surprising, then, that James M. Brewbaker reported recently in *English Journal* (the professional publication of the National Council of Teachers of English), that "thoughtfully conservative" analysts of young adult fiction typically used in secondary schools will likely conclude that such books, "taken together, teach, between the lines, that religion is not very important, that a handicap or divorce or rape or even a parent's death can be dealt with in purely secular terms." Brewbaker does cite a few textbooks (five out of thirty-four) that, he says, offer a strong "religious context." But even in these cases, he concedes that the emphasis on adolescent doubt, despair, and the occult will offend "some conservative critics." ("Our Father which art in Hell," prays the suicidal protagonist in one of these allegedly more religious works.)[10]

But to fully understand the contemporary literary assault upon religion, it is necessary to look back at the origins of academic study of English literature (a relatively new school subject). Thomas Carlyle exemplified the nineteenth century Romantic attitude when he identified his work as a "new Bible" and heralded the "Guild of Authors" as the "Popes" and "Bishops" of a new "true Church" in which communicants would be offered something better than the "putrid heaps of lies" preached in the existing denominations.[11]

Most of the scholars and critics who first defined English literature as an academic discipline largely shared Carlyle's view of literature. Matthew Arnold, a leader of those who created the new discipline, explicitly stated that he wanted poetry taught in the schools as a quasi-religious replacement for the fading "shadows and dreams" of creedal Christianity.[12] The influential "Newbolt Report" prepared in England shortly after World War I urged literature teachers to make of their subject "one of the chief temples of the human spirit, in which all should worship."[13]

Manifesting the continuing sway of this kind of thinking within the discipline is the recent declaration by leading American critic, novelist, and scholar Joyce Carol Oates, that "for both the collective and individual *salvation* of the race, art is more important than anything else, and literature most important of all." But, of course, the salvific literature Oates endorses must fully repudiate the "fantastical spirit-world of wistful and childlike yearnings" found in "traditional religion."[14] Indeed, ironically, Carlyle's vision of the establishment of a new non-Chrsitian "true Church" of creative literature has largely been fulfilled in the public literature classes of a country which prides itself on having no state-established church. American high schools offer relatively few Bible-as-literature courses, but they do offer hundreds of literature-as-Bible courses.

What the vaunted "separation of church and state" has in practice often meant in the American literature classroom is the almost systematic exclusion of those literary works and critical approaches informed by religious conviction. Representative is "A Symposium on Pre-1900 Classics Worth Using in School" (the very title of the symposium suggests strongly pro-modernist bias) published in the *English Journal*. While classical religion found expression in three works (*The Odyssey, Antigone,* and Shakespeare's *Julius Caesar*), the only pre-1900 Christian work cited was the engaging but not profound *Ivanhoe* by Sir Walter Scott.[15] "Milton! Thou shouldst be living at this hour," indeed. What has apparently happened is that Plato's understanding of the public function of poetry has been entirely inverted: hymns are now the poetic works most likely to be kept *out* of the republic's classrooms.

Edmund Gosse, who worked with Arnold as an early exponent of English literature as an academic subject, admitted that the new subject could only be maintained in a place of public prominence "by an effort of bluff on the part of a small influential class."[16] Perhaps this bluff was unobjectionable thirty or forty years ago when literary curriculums almost always allowed for ample consideration of the religious art of such writers as Milton, Bunyan, or Herbert. However, since literature study has now often become a vehicle for attacking scriptural faith, it may be time for devout American parents and taxpayers to seriously question the literary "bluff."

Surely, a public education without training in imaginative literature of any sort would be a deplorably narrow one. And, too, a public literature course consisting of nothing but hymns, devotional poetry, and religious fiction would be terribly contracted. But confronted with a bias favoring irreligious and antireligious literature and critical approaches, for antiprayers and antisermons, millions of American taxpayers might prefer not to continue their support for a Carlylean "true Church" of Authors. For in many of its contemporary American chapels, that church is one that, to borrow a line from Shakespeare, "has no relish of salvation in't."

Notes to Appendix B

1. G.K. Chesterton, *The Victorian Age in Literature* (New York: Oxford University Press, 1947), pp. 89-90; Ifor Evans, *A Short History of English Literature*, rev. ed. (Baltimore: Penguin, 1963), pp. 194-95.
2. William Empson, *Milton's God*, rev. ed. (London: Chatto J. Windus, 1965), pp. 229-37; C.S. Lewis, *A Preface to 'Paradise Lost'* (London: Oxford University Press, 1942), pp. 89-90.
3. Stevens quoted by Richard John Neuhaus, *Freedom for Ministry* (New York: Harper & Row, 1979), p. 44.
4. Plato, *The Republic*, trans. B. Jewett (New York: Modern Library, n.d.), bk X, pp. 377-78.
5. Samuel Johnson, *Rasselas, Poems, and Selected Prose*, ed. Bertrand H. Bronson (New York: Holt, Rinehart & Winston, 1958), chap. X, p. 527.
6. Leo Tolstoy, *What Is Art?* trans. Almyer Maude (Indianapolis: Bobbs-Merrill, 1960), p. 54.
7. T.S. Eliot, *Selected Essays*, 2nd ed. (New York: Harcourt, Brace, & World, 1950), p. 343.
8. Flannery O'Connor, *Mystery and Manners*, eds. Sally and Robert Fitzgerald (New York: Farrar, Straus, & Giroux, 1969), p. 140.
9. Robert E. Spiller, *The Cycle of American Literature: An Essay in Historical Criticism* (New York: Free Press, 1967), p. 229.
10. James W. Brewbaker, *English Journal*, Sept. 1983, pp. 82-86.
11. See *Two Note Books of Thomas Carlyle*, ed. Charles E. Norton (New York: Grolier Club, 1898), pp. 263-64; *The Collected Letters of Thomas and Jane Welsh Carlyle*, Duke-Edinburgh Edition, eds. Charles R. Sanders and Kenneth J. Fielding (Durham: Duke University Press, 1970-81), 5:136; Fred Kaplan, *Thomas Carlyle* (Ithaca: Cornell University Press, 1983), p. 530.
12. Matthew Arnold, "The Study of Poetry," *Essays in Criticism: Second Series* (1888; rpt. London: Macmillan, 1902), pp. 1-3.
13. Newbolt Report quoted by Chris Baldick, *The Social Mission of English Criticism, 1848-1932* (Oxford: Clarendon Press, 1983), p. 97.
14. Joyce Carol Oates, *The Profane Art* (New York: E.P. Dutton, 1983), pp. 37, 187-89.
15. Bonnie Harens, Larry Crapse, et al., "A Symposium on Pre-1900 Classics Worth Using in School," *English Journal*, March 1983, pp. 51-57.
16. Gosse quoted by Baldick, *The Social Mission of English Criticism*, p. 230.

Appendix C

Resources for Changing
the School Situation

The following is a partial list of books and organizations. More belong
on each list, and the number is growing.

Part I: Books

Arons, Stephen. *Compelling Belief: The Culture of American Schooling.*
New York: McGraw-Hill, 1983. (Paperback now available from the
University of Massachusetts Press. Amherst, MA). An outstanding
interpretation by a legal scholar of government schools as a violation
of the Constitution's First Amendment.

Blumenfeld, Samuel L. *Is Public Education Necessary?* Old Greenwich,
CT: Devin-Adair, 1981. A little-appreciated historical eye-opener
showing the statist and antireligious bias in the public schools since
their founding by Horace Mann. The early material is especially
important.

Blumenfeld, Samuel L. *NEA: Trojan Horse in American Education.* Boise,
ID: Paradigm, 1984. A thoroughly documented critique of the
NEA's hidden and not-so-hidden agenda for America's public
schools.

Coons, John E., and Stephen D. Sugarman. *Education by Choice: The Case
for Family Control.* Berkeley, CA: University of California Press,
1978. One of the first extensive discussions of the legal and
philosophical case for tuition vouchers.

Everhart, Robert B., ed. *The Public School Monopoly: A Critical Analysis of
Education and the State in American Society.* San Francisco, CA:
Ballinger (of Harper & Row). A group of scholarly essays dealing
with many of the issues raised by monopoly government schools.

Gabler, Mel and Norman (with James C. Hefley). *What Are They
Teaching Our Children?* Wheaton, IL: SP Publications, 1985. An
extensive treatment of the many kinds of bias in school textbooks by
the pioneers in textbooks evaluations.

Gow, Kathleen M. *Yes, Virginia There Is Right and Wrong.* Wheaton, IL:
Tyndale, 1985. (First published 1980, McGraw-Hill). Treatment of

the biased and confused approaches to values in the public schools.

London, Herbert I. *Why Are They Lying to Our Children?* New York: Stein and Day, 1984. A book-length treatment of the pro-ecology and antieconomic growth position, with the negative portrayal of the future found so often in public school textbooks.

McCarthy, Rockne M., Donald Oppewal, Walfred Peterson, and Gordon Spykman. *Society, State and Schools: A Case for Structural and Confessional Pluralism.* Grand Rapids, MI: Eerdmans, 1981.

McCarthy, Rockne M., James W. Skillen, and William A. Harper. *Disestablishment a Second Time.* Grand Rapids, MI: Christian College Consortium and W.B. Eerdmans, 1982. Two extensive, scholarly treatments of the essential sectarianism of the public schools. Very good historical treatments of American political and educational philosophy and their implications for understanding the present unsatisfactory character of the public schools.

McLaughlin, Sister Raymond. *The Liberty of Choice: Freedom and Justice in Education.* Collegeville, MN: The Liturgical Press, 1979. Summaries of how other major Western democracies settled the school conflict from a Catholic perspective.

Reed, Sally D. *NEA: Propaganda Front of the Radical Left.* (No place or publisher listed), 1984. An easily readable indictment of the NEA, but without documentation.

Schlafly, Phyllis (Ed), *Child Abuse in the Classroom.* (Alson, Illinois: Marquette Press, 1984.) Detailed testimonies of American parents to government officials about what is wrong with our public (government) schools.

Part II: Organizations

American Education Report, 721 Second Street, N.E., Washington, D.C. 20002.

California Monitor of Education, Box 402, Alamo, CA 94507.

Educational Freedom, 20 Parkland, Glendale, MO 63122.

Educational Choice, 1611 Norton Kent Street, Suite 805, Arlington, VA 22209.

Appendix D

Table D-1

The Sixty Social Studies Books in the Sample
Listed by Publisher, Grade, and Title

(Authors are not listed since some books had no official
author(s), others listed Senior and Junior authors,
others consultants, project directors, etc.)

1. American Book: 1982
- Grade 1   *People*
- Grade 2   *Neighbors*
- Grade 3   *Places*
- Grade 4   *People in Places*
- Grade 5   *The American People*
- Grade 6   *People of the World*

2. Allyn & Bacon: 1983
- Grade 1   *Home and School*
- Grade 2   *People in Neighborhoods*
- Grade 3   *Our Communities*
- Grade 4   *World Regions*
- Grade 5   *Our United States*
- Grade 6   *People, Time and Change*

3. Holt, Rinehart & Winston: 1983
- Grade 1   *People*
- Grade 2   *Neighborhoods*
- Grade 3   *Communities*
- Grade 4   *Our Regions*
- Grade 5   *Our History*
- Grade 6   *Our World*

4. Laidlaw (Doubleday): 1983
- Grade 1   *Understanding People*
- Grade 2   *Understanding Families*
- Grade 3   *Understanding Communities*
- Grade 4   *Understanding Regions of the Earth*
- Grade 5   *Understanding Our Country*
- Grade 6   *Understanding the World*

5. McGraw-Hill: 1983
- Grade 1   *Meeting People*
- Grade 2   *Going Places*

Grade 3 *Communities*
Grade 4 *Earth's Regions*
Grade 5 *United States*
Grade 6 *The World*

6. Macmillan: 1982-83
Grade 1 *Families and Friends* 1983
Grade 2 *People and Neighborhoods* 1983
Grade 3 *Communities—Today and Yesterday* 1983
Grade 4 *The Earth and Its People* 1983
Grade 5 *The United States and Other Americas* 1982
Grade 6 *Nations of the World* 1982

7. Riverside: 1982
Grade 1 *You and Me*
Grade 2 *Here We Are*
Grade 3 *Our Land*
Grade 4 *Where on Earth*
Grade 5 *The Americans*
Grade 6 *The World Now and Then*

8. Scott, Foresman: 1983
Grade 1 *Families and Friends*
Grade 2 *Neighbors Near and Far*
Grade 3 *City, Town, and Country*
Grade 4 *Regions of Our Country and Our World*
Grade 5 *America Past and Present*
Grade 6 *Our World: Land and Cultures*

9. Silver Burdett: 1984
Grade 1 *Families and Neighborhoods*
Grade 2 *Neighborhoods and Communities*
Grade 3 *Communities and Resources*
Grade 4 *States and Regions*
Grade 5 *The United States and Its People*
Grade 6 *The World and Its People: Europe, Africa, Asia and Australia (Scholastic)*

10. Steck-Vaughn: 1983
Grade 1 *Our Families*
Grade 2 *Our Neighborhoods*
Grade 3 *Our Communities*
Grade 4 *Our Country Today*
Grade 5 *Our Country's History*
Grade 6 *Our World Today*

Table D-2

Secondary References to Religion in Social Studies Textbooks Grades 1-4
(American references only)

Book (publisher)	Grade 1 Text	Grade 1 Image
1. American Book		
2. Allyn & Bacon		
3. Holt, Rinehart & Winston		Christmas tree (no religious aspects)
4. Laidlaw		
5. Macmillan	Pledge of Allegiance	Church on map; picture: Rev. M.L. King
6. McGraw-Hill		Image Map "house of worship"

Grade 2		Grade 3		Grade 4	
Text	Image	Text	Image	Text	Image
	Amish; three churches in drawings	Pilgrims not allowed to pray in own way			Church building on colonial town map
		Sp. built mission churches			
	Church building on colonial town map	Pilgrims came for religious reasons; worshipped every Sunday	two mission churches	Puritans: rel. free.; Puritan: church control; Wm. Penn: Quaker, rel. free.; M. Anderson: young in ch. choir; Sp. missionaries; N. Whitman: pioneer missionary, woman.	Mission churches (3)
Pledge Flag	Wedding party and cross	Religious community leaders, important serv. worker	Amish; Sp. Mission; Hse. of Buddha in Chinatown		
"America the Beautiful"	photo of church	Colonial "Lords Prayer"; town has churches; M.L. King a minister	Spanish Mission; Roman Catholic cathedral	Pledge of Allegiance	
Church "a group"; symbol for church and synagogue on map		Mission; religion and early settlers		Roger Williams; Anne Hutchinson	

7. Riverside	Crucifix in background
8. Scott, Foresman	Pilgrims and Bradford wanted to pray in own way
9. Silver Burdett	
10. Steck-Vaughn/ Scholastic	Christmas tree; Easter egg (neither religious)

	Church in town plan; Pilgrims in rel. service			
Pledge of Allegiance; right to pray	Story on Amish; El Barrio story; rel. free. Brewster, Puritans, Huchinson.; churches help in flood	Grt. Seal of U.S.	Huguenots rel. free.; Spanish built churches, spread Christianity, no longer allowed Indians to practice their religion. Explain B.C./A.D.	Span. missions (2); Mormon temple
	Jewish Israel parade; Pledge of Allegiance	Place of worship on map; Pledge of Allegiance		
	Draw. of neighborhood has small church, wedding party outside; church on map (same map 4X); photo of church	Mormons settled Utah; Fr. Serra and Calif. missions	Mormon temple	

Table D-3

Family Emphasis in Social Studies Texts—Grades 1-4

Textbook Publisher	No Emphasis: zero pages on family	Slight Emphasis: 1-5 pages on family
1. American Book 1982		Grade 4
2. Allyn & Bacon 1983	Grade 2 Grade 4	
3. Holt, Rinehart & Winston 1983	Grade 4	Grade 3
4. Laidlaw 1983	Grade 1 Grade 3 Grade 4	
5. Macmillan 1982-83		Grade 4
6. McGraw-Hill 1983		Grade 3 Grade 4
7. Riverside 1982	Grade 3	Grade 2 Grade 4
8. Scott, Foresman 1983	Grade 3 Grade 4	
9. Silver Burdett 1984	Grade 4	Grade 2 Grade 3
10. Steck-Vaughn 1983		

Moderate Emphasis: 6-15 pages on family	Strong Emphasis: 16-25 pages on family	Very Strong Emphasis: more than 25 on family
Grade 1 Grade 2 Grade 3		
Grade 1	Grade 3	
	Grade 2	Grade 1
		Grade 2
Grade 2	Grade 1	Grade 3
	Grade 1 Grade 2	
Grade 1		
Grade 1 Grade 2		
	Grade 1	
	Grade 2 Grade 4	Grade 1 Grade 3

Notes

Chapter Two

1. *Textbook Adoptions 1983-84.* (Sacramento, CA: Office of Curriculum Framework and Textbook Development, State Department of Education, 1983); *Textbooks, Current—Adoption 1982-1983.* (Austin, TX: Texas Education Agency, 1982).
2. *Catalog of State-Adopted Instructional Material 1983-84.* (Tallahassee, FL: State of Florida, Department of Education, 1983); *The Georgia Textbook List 1983.* (Atlanta, GA: Georgia Department of Education, Textbooks and Title IV Local System Support Division).
3. Statistics from *Digest of Educational Statistics.* (Washington, D.C.: U.S. Government Printing Office, 1982). Based on 1981 statistics.
4. Frances FitzGerald, *America Revised. History Schoolbooks in the Twentieth Century.* (Boston: Little, Brown, 1979, p. 19ff); Arthur Woodward, *Taking Teaching out of Teaching and Reading out of Learning to Read—A Historical Study of Reading Textbook Teachers Guides 1920-1980.* (Paper presented at the Annual Meeting of the American Educational Research Association, April 1985).
5. Letter to the author, November 15, 1985.

Chapter Four

1. Alexis de Tocqueville, *Democracy in America,* J.P. Mayer, ed., trans. G. Lawrence, (Garden City, NY: Doubleday, 1969, pp. 295 and 292).
2. Robert Bryan, *History, Pseudo-History, Anti-History: How Public School Textbooks Treat Religion* (Washington, D.C.: Learn, Inc. The Education Foundation, ca. 1984).
3. Ibid., p. 2.
4. Ibid.
5. Ibid., pp. 3, 10.
6. Ibid., p. 4.

Chapter Five

1. Christopher Lasch, *The Culture of Narcissism* (New York: Norton, 1978).

Chapter Six

1. Barbara Cohen, "Censoring the Sources," *School Library Journal* (March 1986).

2. Ibid., p. 97.
3. Ibid., p. 98.
4. Ibid.
5. Ibid., p. 99.
6. Ibid.
7. Ibid.
8. This is also the opinion of Mel and Norma Gabler in *What Are They Teaching Our Children* (Wheaton, IL: SP Publications, 1985).
9. From American Publishers Industry Statistics, 1982, plus 6 percent inflation adjustments for 1983-1985. Statistics supplied by EPIE (Data for elementary and high school textbooks).
10. For example, Arthur Woodward, David L. Elliott, and Kathleen Carter Nagel, "Beyond Textbooks in Elementary Social Studies," *Social Education,* January 1986, pp. 50-53; David L. Elliott, Kathleen Carter Nagel, and Arthur Woodward, *A Study of Elementary Social Studies Series.* Unpublished report (New York: EPIE Institute, Teachers College, Columbia University, December 1984); Harriet Tyson-Bernstein and Arthur Woodward, "The Great Textbook Machine and Prospects for Reform," *Social Education* (January 1986), pp. 41-45.
11. For a discussion of these reforms see Diane Ravitch, *The Troubled Crusade: American Education 1945-1980* (New York: Basic, 1983).
12. Peter Brimelow, "What to Do About America's Schools," *Fortune* (19 September, 1983), pp. 60-64.
13. Joseph Adelson, "What Happened to the Schools," *Commentary* (March 1981), pp. 36-41.
14. Ibid., p. 37.
15. Ibid.
16. Ibid.
17. Ibid.
18. Ibid., p. 38.
19. Dewey's central role in the first *Humanist Manifesto* is well known. See D.L. Cuddy, "How American Education was Misdirected," *Lincoln Review,* 6 (1985), p. 43.
20. Skinner signed the *Humanist Manifesto II;* for Rogers as a humanist, see Paul C. Vitz, *Psychology as Religion: The Cult of Self-Worship* (Grand Rapids, MI: Eerdmans, 1977).
21. E.g., Lawrence Kohlberg, in *The Humanist* (November/December 1978), pp. 13-15.
22. See, for example, Richard Baer, "Values Clarification as Indoctrination", *The Educational Forum,* 41, (1977), pp. 155-165; also Paul C. Vitz, *Values Clarification: A Critical Summary* (1985). Unpublished report for the Department of Education (available from the author).
23. *The Connecticut Mutual Life Report on American Values in the 80s: The Impact of Belief* (Hartford, CT: Connecticut Mutual Life Insurance Co., 1981).
24. Ibid., p. 219, Table 136.
25. Ibid., pp. 220-221, Tables 138, 139.

26. Ibid., pp. 219-223, Tables 135-144.
27. For the NEA's influence and political philosophy, see Samuel L. Blumenfeld, *NEA: Trojan Horse in American Education* (Boise, ID: Paradigm, 1984).
28. *Connecticut Mutual Life Report,* p. 252.
29. Thomas Jefferson.
30. Stephen Arons, *Compelling Belief: The Culture of American Schooling* (New York: McGraw-Hill, 1983).
31. Ibid., pp. 204-205.
32. A Gallup Poll, 1985, on education found that minority respondents favor education vouchers by 59% to 26%.
33. Arons, p. 211.
34. See especially Rockne M. McCarthy, Donald Oppewal, Walfred Peterson, and Gordon Spykman, *Society, State and Schools* (Grand Rapids, MI: Eerdmans, 1981); Rockne M. McCarthy, James W. Skillen, and William A. Harper, *Disestablishment a Second Time: Genuine Pluralism for American Schools* (Grand Rapids, MI: Christian College Consortium and W.B. Eerdman, 1982).
35. See Samuel L. Blumenfeld, *Is Public Education Necessary?* (Old Greenwich, CT: Devin-Adair, 1981).
36. Joseph Berger, "Day School Urged for Reform Jews," *New York Times* (November 5, 1985), p. A13.
37. For evidence of the growth of home schooling, contact The Home School Legal Defense Association, P.O. Box 2091, Washington, D.C. 20013.
38. John Coons and Stephen Sugarman, *Family Choice in Education* (Berkeley, CA: University of California Press, 1982).
39. Robert B. Everhart, ed. *The Public School Monopoly: A Critical Analysis of Education and the State in American Society* (San Francisco, CA: Ballinger Publishing Company, 1983).
40. Sr. Raymond McLaughlin, *The Liberty of Choice: Freedom and Justice in Education* (Collegeville, MN: The Liturgical Press, 1979).
41. Ibid., p. 125.
42. Ibid.
43. Ibid., p. 126.
44. Ibid., pp. 121-122.
45. Ibid., p. 129.
46. James S. Coleman, *Schools, Families, and Children,* The 1985 Ryerson Lecture, The University of Chicago, (April 24, 1985), p. 20.

Bibliography

"A Statement Affirming Evolution as a Principle of Science." *The Humanist* (January-February, 1977), p. 4.

Bird, Wendell. "Freedom of Religion and Science Instruction in Public Schools." *The Yale Journal* 78: 521-2.

Bryan, Robert. *History, Pseudo-History, Anti-History: How Public School Textbooks Treat Religion.* Washington, D.C.: Policy Studies in Education, Learn, Inc., n.d.

Bucher, Charles. *Health.* New Jersey: Silver Burdett Co., 1981.

Cangemi, Jo Ann, ed. 1983. *Holt Social Studies: Our World.* New York: Holt, Rinehart & Winston.

Dow, Peter. "MACOS: The Study of Human Behavior as One Road to Survival." *Phi Delta Kappan* (October, 1975).

Dow, Peter. *Talks to Teachers.* Cambridge, Mass.: Education Development Center, 1970.

Gall, Meredith. *Evaluating and Selecting Curriculum Materials.* Boston: Allyn & Bacon, 1981.

Gordon, E., ed. 1975. *Introduction to Literature.* Lexington, Mass.: Ginn and Company.

Hillocks, George. "Books and Bombs: Ideological Conflict and the Schools." *School Review* (August, 1978).

Humanist Manifesto I and *II.* Buffalo, New York: Prometheus Press, 1976.

Hurd, Paul. "An Exploratory Study of the Impact of BSCS Secondary School Curriculum Materials." *American Biology Teacher* 38 (1976): 80 ff.

James, M. et al. "Social Issues Serve as Unifying Theme in a Biology Course." *American Biology Teacher* 36 (1974): 346-348. Kieffer, M. "Future Planning: Biology, Society an Ethical Education." *The Science Teacher* 42 (1975): 10-12.

LaPlace, John. *Health.* 3rd ed. Englewood Cliffs, New Jersey: Prentice-Hall, 1980.

Le Fever, Ernest, ed. *Values in an American Government Textbook.* Washington, D.C.: Public Policy Center, Georgetown University, 1978.

Leven, Florence and Joy Lindbeck. "An Analysis of Selected Biology Texts for the Treatment of Controversial Issues and Biosocial Problems." *Journal of Research In Science Teaching* 16, No. 3 (1979): 199-203.

McCarthy, Rockne, et al. *Society, State, and Schools: A Case For Structural and Confessional Pluralism.* Grand Rapids, MI: Eerdmans Publishing Company, 1981.

Marshner, Susan. *Man: A Course of Study—Prototype for Federalized Textbooks?* Washington, D.C.: Heritage Foundation, Inc., 1975.

McFarlund, P., et al., eds. 1972. *Themes in American Literature.* Boston, Mass.: Houghton Mifflin Co.

McNearney, Clayton. "The Kanawha County Textbook Controversy," *Religious Education* (September-October, 1975).

Pengalley, Eric. *Sex and Human Life.* Menlo Park, CA: Addison-Wesley, 1974.

Pflug, Harold. "Religion in Missouri Textbooks." *Phi Delta Kappan* (April, 1955).

Schmidt, James and J. Conley. "Social Issues Serve as Unifying Theme in a Biology Course." *American Biology Teacher,* 36 (1974): 346-8.

Sonneborn, M. "Secondary School Preparation for Making Biological Decisions." *NASSP Bulletin* 56 (1972): 1-12.

Todd, Lewis and Merle Curti. *Rise of the American Nation.* New York: Harcourt Brace Jovanovich, 1972.

Welch, Betty. *Introduction to Literature* and *Teacher's Handbook and Key.* Lexington, Mass.: Ginn and Company, 1975.

Weitzman, D. and R. Gross. *The Human Experience: World Culture Series.* Boston: Houghton Mifflin Co., 1974.

Other Books
of Interest

The Seduction of Society
Pornography and Its Impact on American Life
By William A. Stanmeyer

A constitutional scholar and lawyer addresses what can be done about the pornography crisis. $5.95

Whose Values?
The Battle for Morality in Pluralistic America
Edited by Carl Horn

Paul Vitz, William Ball, James Hitchcock, Joseph Sobran, Terry Eastland, and others examine the major issues of our time: secular humanism, the breakdown of the family, abortion and infanticide, the crisis in education, and the role of public policy. $8.95

The Zero People
Edited by Jeff Hensley
A comprehensive view of the assault on human life today—through abortion, infanticide, and euthanasia. Contributions by John Powell, C. Everett Koop, Malcolm Muggeridge, Michael Novak, George Will, Harold O.J. Brown, and Pope John Paul II. $7.95

Available at your Christian Bookstore or from:
Servant Publications • **Dept. 209** • **P.O. Box 7455**
Ann Arbor, Michigan 48107
Please include payment plus $.75 for postage.
Send for our FREE catalog of Christian
books, music, and cassettes.